Herbert Puchta and Jeff Stranks

English in Mind

* Student's Book 1

CAMBRIDGE
UNIVERSITY PRESS

Speaking & Functions	Listening	Reading	Writing
Expressing likes & dislikes	Interviews about hobbies	An unusual hobby Story: Different – so what?	Letter about your hobbies
Talking about regular activities Talking about school subjects	Dialogue about a school timetable	At home – at school Culture: A school in Britain	Description of your usual school day
Talking about activities happening now Talking about housework	Radio interview with a volunteer in Belize	Hard work and no money Story: Where's Amy going?	Email about organising a party
Expressing quantity Ordering food Talking about food & fitness	Restaurant dialogue	Getting fat or keeping fit? Culture: What *is* British food?	Paragraph about food & fitness
Talking about the past Talking about when/where you were born	Presentation on 'My hero'	The woman who lived in a tree Story: Who's your hero?	Poster about your hero
Asking about the past Re-telling a story	Television comedy story	The start of a great friendship Culture: Using mobile phones	Email about an enjoyable day/weekend
Talking about obligations Describing job requirements	Presentation on success Descriptions of future jobs	Why are they so successful? The 1900 House Story: It's my dream	Description of a job
Talking about non-specific amounts Talking about possession Talking about sleep & dreams	Song: *What Makes You Think They're Happy?*	4Tune's new music Dreaming up new ideas Culture: Pop idols	Imaginative story
Comparing things	Descriptions & interview about language learning	More than one language Amazing facts – or just lies? Story: I have to bounce!	Description or letter/email about language learning
Talking about arrangements Discussing holiday plans	Dialogues about holiday plans	Welcome to Ireland Culture: Adventure holiday in paradise	Magazine article about a class trip
Making predictions Talking about your future life	Science fiction story Future predictions Song: *Space Oddity*	Dialogue from a science fiction story Story: How embarrassing!	Competition entry about your life in the future
Describing the weather Giving advice Describing actions	Dialogue about the life of Wilma Rudolph	We can't give up! Culture: New Americans	Email giving advice to a friend
Talking about intentions	Dialogue about New Year's resolutions Dialogue about an unlucky day	New Year's resolutions Story: A birthday party	Email about New Year's Eve
Giving advice & recommendations Planning a friend's visit	Information about different customs	Quiz: Other cultures Culture: Tips for the tourist in Britain	Letter/Email giving tips to a tourist
Expressing future possibilities Telling a story	Dialogues about bravery	Face-to-face with a gorilla Story: Dave's risk	Re-telling a story about facing danger
Talking about life experiences Talking about things you've done / never done	Interview about strange pets	Have you ever seen anything like it? John Evans, the Headbalancer Culture: Elvis lives	Letter/Email about a visit to Los Angeles

Starter section

 A Nice to meet you

1 Greetings and introductions

a 🔊 Complete the dialogue with the words in the box. Then listen and check.

> fine   I'm   ~~name's~~   Nice   this   you

Liz: Hi. My ¹ _name's_ Liz.
Monica: Hello, Liz. ² _____ Monica.
Liz: Oh, hi, Jack. How are you?
Jack: I'm ³ _____ , thanks. How about ⁴ _____ ?
Liz: OK, thanks. Monica, ⁵ _____ is my friend, Jack.
Monica: ⁶ _____ to meet you.
Jack: Hi, Monica.

b Work in a group of three. Have conversations like the one in Exercise 1a.

> **Remember**
>
> My name's ... (*I* → *my*)   What's your name? (*you* → *your*)

2 Countries and nationalities

a 🔊 Write the names of the countries. Then listen and check.

> Argentina   Belgium   Brazil   ~~Britain~~
> Canada   China   France   Germany
> Italy   Japan   Poland   Russia
> Spain   Switzerland   Turkey   USA

1 _Britain_   9 _____
2 _____   10 _____
3 _____   11 _____
4 _____   12 _____
5 _____   13 _____
6 _____   14 _____
7 _____   15 _____
8 _____   16 _____

b Work with a partner. Write the nationalities for the countries in Exercise 2a.

-an/-ian	Argentinian Belgian
-ish	British
others	Chinese French

3 The verb *be*

Positive	Negative	Question	Short answer
I'm (am)	I'm not (am not)	Am I ...?	Yes, I **am**. No, I'm **not**.
you/we 're (are)	you/we/they **aren't**	Are you/we/they ...?	Yes, you/we/they **are**. No, you/we/they **aren't**.
he/she/it 's (is)	he/she/it **isn't**	Is he/she/it ...?	Yes, he/she/it **is**. No, he/she/it **isn't**.

Remember:
personal pronouns

Singular:
I   you   he, she, it
Plural:
we   you   they

a Fill in the spaces with the correct form of *be* (positive or negative).

1 You *'re* from Italy!

2 He _____ from Turkey.

3 She _____ Italian.

4 We _____ from Argentina.

5 It _____ British.

6 They _____ from Japan.

b ◁)) Complete the dialogue with the correct form of the verb *be*. Then listen and check.

Jack: Hi. My name ¹ *'s* Jack, and this ² _____ Monica. She ³ _____ from Italy.

Marek: Nice to meet you. I ⁴ _____ Marek, and those two people ⁵ _____ my friends, Barbara and Adam. ⁶ _____ you from Rome, Monica?

Monica: No, I ⁷ _____ from Milan. Where ⁸ _____ you from?

Marek: We ⁹ _____ from Poland. Adam and I ¹⁰ _____ from Warsaw and Barbara ¹¹ _____ from Gdansk. ¹² _____ you on holiday in Cambridge?

Monica: No, I ¹³ _____ not. I'm a student at a language school here. ¹⁴ _____ you all students?

Marek: Yes, we ¹⁵ _____ . We ¹⁶ _____ at a language school too.

c Work with a partner. Ask and answer questions about the people in Exercise 3b.

A: *Is Monica from Poland?*
B: *No, she **isn't**. She's from Milan, in Italy. **Are** Marek and Adam ...?*

B Personal information

1 Numbers

a 🔊 Write the missing numbers. Then listen and repeat.

1	*one*	11	eleven
2	two	12	....
3	....	13	thirteen
4	four	14	....
5	....	15	fifteen
6	six	16	....
7	....	17	seventeen
8	eight	18	....
9	....	19	nineteen
10	ten	20	twenty

b 🔊 Listen and repeat these numbers.

21	twenty-one	60	sixty
22	twenty-two	70	seventy
25	twenty-five	80	eighty
29	twenty-nine	90	ninety
30	thirty	100	a hundred
40	forty	1,000	a thousand
50	fifty		

c 🔊 Listen and circle the number you hear.

1 (17) 70
2 19 90
3 64 46
4 42 52
5 71 79
6 28 38

d Work with a partner. Ask and answer.

A: *How old are you?*
B: *I'm fourteen. How old is your brother?*
A: *He's twenty-one. How old ...?*

Remember

How old	are	you?
	are	they?
	is	he/she/it?

2 Titles

Fill in the spaces with *Mr, Mrs, Miss* or *Ms*.

①

Good morning, Mike.

Hello, ... Wilson.

②

Hello, Joanna.

Hello, ... Cooper.

③

Title (Mr / Mrs / Ms)
....

④

Please take a seat, ... Anderson.

3 The alphabet

a 🔊 Listen and repeat the letters.
Then write the letters under the sounds.

/eɪ/	/iː/	/e/	/aɪ/	/əʊ/	/uː/	/ ɑː/
_a_	_b_	_f_	_i_	_o_	_q_	_r_
....	....	....	....		....	
....	....	....			....	
....	....	....				
	....	....				
	....	....				
	....	....				
	....					

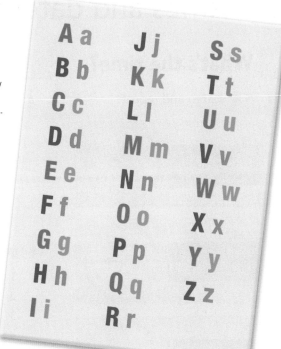

b How do you spell numbers?
Ask and answer with a partner.

A: *How do you spell* three?
B: *T-H-R-E-E. How do you spell* twelve?

4 Giving your personal information

a Complete the form with your personal information.

WESTBOURNE CITY LIBRARY

Family name		First name	
Address			
		Postcode	
Telephone		Email	
Age		Male ☐ Female ☐	

c Put the words in order
to make questions.

1 your / What's / name
   What's your name?
2 spell / How / it / you / do
   .... ?
3 address / your / What's
   .... ?
4 you / old / are / How
   .... ?
5 number / What's / phone / your
   .... ?

d Work with a partner. Ask and
answer the questions in Exercise 4c.
Write your partner's answers.

b 🔊 Listen to the phone conversation and correct the
information on the form. There is one mistake in each line.

Hartfield Sports Centre

First name ~~Francis~~ *Frances*

Family name Tomson

Address 27 Grove Street, Hartfield

Telephone number 0982 637410

Age 15

C Times and dates

1 What's the time?

a 🔊 Listen and repeat.

Remember

To ask about times, use
What time ...? or *When ...?*
What time is your music lesson?
When is your music lesson?

b Look at the clocks and say the times.

Eleven o'clock.

2 Days of the week

a 🔊 Put the letters in order to write the days of the week. Then listen and repeat.

~~drifay~~   shutyard   trasuyad   dmonya   dyasnu
yaddewnse   sdatuye

M	T	W	T	F	S	S
....	....	....	....	*Friday*	....	....

b Answer the questions.

1 What day is it today? ....
2 What day is it tomorrow? ....
3 When is your next English lesson? ....
4 What's your favourite day of the week? ....

3 Months and seasons

a 🔊 Put the months in order (1–12). Then listen and check.

☐ August	☐ October	☐ July	☐ September
1 January	☐ December	☐ May	☐ November
☐ April	☐ February	☐ June	☐ March

b 🔊 Listen again. Mark the main stress in each month, for example: <u>Ja</u>nuary.

c Match the names of the seasons with the pictures.

1 spring   2 summer   3 autumn   4 winter

a

b

c

d

d Which months are in each season in your country? What's your favourite season? Why?

4 Dates

a 🔊 Listen and repeat.

1st first   **2nd** second   **3rd** third   **4th** fourth   **5th** fifth   **6th** sixth   **7th** seventh   **8th** eighth
9th ninth   **10th** tenth   **11th** eleventh   **12th** twelfth   **13th** thirteenth   **15th** fifteenth
18th eighteenth   **20th** twentieth   **21st** twenty-first   **22nd** twenty-second   **23rd** twenty-third

b 🔊 Listen and write the numbers.

1   _3rd_   2   3   ....

4   5   6   ....

c Work with a partner. Ask and answer questions about the months.

A: *What's the first month?*   B: *January. What's the eighth month?*

> **Remember**
>
> **We write:** 8 or 8th December, 2006 or 8/12/06.
>
> **We say:** <u>the</u> eighth <u>of</u> December **or** December <u>the</u> eighth, two thousand and six.

d Look at the pictures and match the three parts of the sentences.

1   Our Science test is on ⟶   the twenty-first   of May.
2   My birthday is on   the fourteenth   of March.
3   The football final is on   the twelfth   of October.
4   Our national holiday is on the fourth   of June.

 14/5

 12/6

 21/10

 4/3

e 🔊 Listen to three dialogues and tick the dates you hear.

1   4th November ☐   14th November ☐
2   13th May ☐   30th May ☐
3   21st August ☐   23rd August ☐

f Say the dates.

1   25/04/2001   *the twenty-fifth of April, two thousand and one*
2   1/8/2001   3   22/3/2010   4   26/2/1997
5   17/11/1999   6   30/5/2005   7   10/7/2000

g Ask other students about their birthday.

When's your birthday?

It's on the twentieth of February.

5 Question words

Complete the questions. Use *What*, *When*, *Where* or *How*.

1   ....'s your name?   5   .... do you spell your name?
2   .... old are you?   6   ....'s the time?
3   .... are you from?   7   ....'s your favourite month?
4   ....'s your birthday?   8   .... are Bill and Jane from?

D At home

1 Colours

Work in a small group. Find something in the classroom for each colour.

It's grey.   They're green.   The wall is yellow.

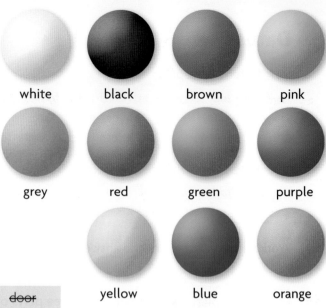

white   black   brown   pink

grey   red   green   purple

yellow   blue   orange

2 Rooms and furniture

a Write the names of the rooms (A–F).

b Label the furniture. Use the words in the box.

armchair bath bed chair cooker cupboard ~~door~~
fridge shower sink sofa table toilet window

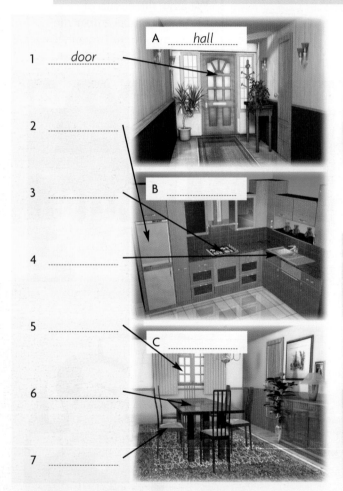

A ___hall___

1 ___door___

2 _____

3 _____

B _____

4 _____

5 _____

C _____

6 _____

7 _____

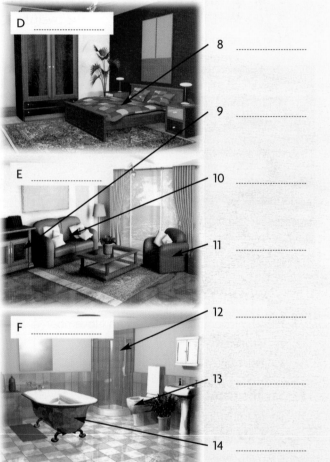

D _____

8 _____

9 _____

E _____

10 _____

11 _____

12 _____

F _____

13 _____

14 _____

3 Plural nouns

Forming plural nouns		Irregular plurals
Add *s*	chair – chairs	man – men
Add *es*	dish – dishes	woman – women
	box – boxes	child – children
	watch – watches	person – people
	address – addresses	
y → ies	dictionary – dictionaries	

Complete the sentences. Use the plural form of the nouns.

1 Two ___policemen___ are at the door. (policeman)
2 There are eight _____ in our street. (family)
3 Our _____ are from Brazil. (friend)
4 My mother is talking to two _____ . (woman)
5 My Maths _____ are in Room 2B. (class)
6 This computer game is for _____ . (child)
7 There are four _____ of _____ in the kitchen. (box, match)

4 There is / There are

There's (There is) a book / an orange.   *There are two books / three oranges.*

a Complete the sentences. Use *There's a/an* or *There are*.

1 .... blue table in the living room.
2 .... two doors.
3 .... orange chair.

4 .... two computers in our house.
5 .... ice cream for you in the fridge.

b Play a memory game. Look at the picture for 30 seconds.
Then make sentences with *There's* or *There are*.

There are two windows.

c Look at the picture again and say where
things are. Use the prepositions in the box.

in	on	under	next to
behind	between		

d Draw a plan of your house/flat. Talk about it
to your partner.

There's a hall, a kitchen, ...
There are three bedrooms.
In the living room there's a green sofa and there are
two brown armchairs.

E In town

1 Shops and businesses

Where can you find or buy the things in the pictures? Write the numbers 1–9 in the boxes.

> 1 ~~bookshop~~   2 cinema   3 café   4 shoe shop
> 5 disco   6 supermarket   7 music shop
> 8 clothes shop   9 post office

a

b

c

d

e

f

g

1

h

i

2 *There is/are* negative and questions + *a/an* or *any*

Positive	Negative	Question	Short answer
There's (There is) a cinema.	There isn't (is not) a cinema.	Is there a cinema?	Yes, there is. No, there isn't (is not).
There are two cinemas.	There aren't any cinemas.	Are there any cinemas?	Yes, there are. No, there aren't (are not).

a 🔊 Listen to Jack talking about his town. Write ✓ (yes) or ✗ (no) in the boxes.

clothes shop ☐   bookshops ☐
schools ☐   supermarket ☐
cafés ☐   discos ☐
music shops ☐   cinema ☐

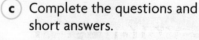

b Match the two parts of each sentence.

1 Are there   a   a good disco in town.
2 Is there   b   a post office here?
3 There aren't   c   any good CDs in the music shop?
4 There's   d   any people in the post office.

c Complete the questions and short answers.

1 A: *Are there any* _____
   bookshops here?
   B: No, there _____ .

2 A: _____
   supermarket in this street?
   B: Yes, _____ .

3 A: _____
   nice clothes in the shop?
   B: Yes, _____ .

4 A: _____
   park in your town?
   B: No, _____ .

d Complete the sentences with *a* or *any*.

1 There aren't .... big shops here.

2 Is there .... post office near here?

3 There's .... good shoe shop in this street.

4 Are there .... discos in this town?

5 There's .... really good music shop over there.

6 There aren't .... trains to London on Sundays.

3 More places in town

a Match the words with the pictures.

> 1 airport   2 sports stadium   3 museum   4 library
> 5 swimming pool   6 university   7 river   8 station

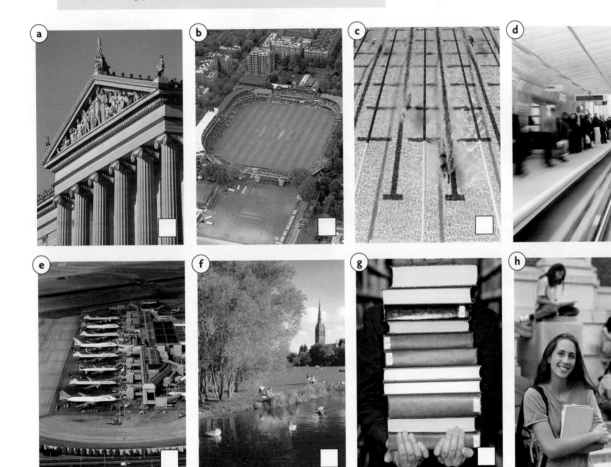

b Work with a partner.
Student A: Look at the information about Langton on this page.
Student B: Turn to page 136 and look at the information about Wendford.

Student A: Ask your partner about these things in Wendford.

cafés   station   discos   library   sports stadium
swimming pools   airport

A: *Are there any cafés?*   B: *Yes, there are .... cafés. / No, there aren't.*
A: *Is there a station?*   B: *Yes, there is. / No, there isn't.*

Student B: Now ask about Langton.

c Would you prefer to live in Langton or Wendford? Why?

d Write about the town where you live. Use *There's / There are* and *There isn't / There aren't*.

Langton info

- no sports stadium
- 4 cafés
- 2 swimming pools
- no library
- 3 discos
- airport
- no station

F Family and friends

1 Members of the family

Label the pictures. Use the words in the box.

~~father~~ grandfather
sister aunt uncle
brother mother
grandmother

1 _____

2 _____

3 _____

4 _____*father*_____

5 _____

6 _____

Stefano

7 _____

8 _____

2 Possessive 's

John's book

my sister's bicycle

my sisters' dog

Complete the sentences. Use the possessive form of the nouns.

1 _*Antonio's*_ computer is great. (Antonio)

2 _____ cats are in the living room. (Susanna)

3 _____ bedroom is next to the bathroom. (My brothers)

4 _____ eyes are blue. (My uncle)

5 _____ name is Miss Watkins. (My teacher)

6 _____ house is very small. (My grandparents)

3 Possessive adjectives

Read Liz's letter from her new penfriend, Laura. Fill in the spaces with *my*, *your*, *his*, *her*, *our* or *their*.

Singular	Plural
I → my	we → our
you → your	you → your
he → his	they → their
she → her	
it → its	

Dear Liz

Thank you very much for ¹ *your* letter and the photos of ² _____ friends and family. ³ _____ mum and dad look really nice in the photo. Now I can tell you about me and ⁴ _____ family here in Switzerland.

I've got two brothers. ⁵ _____ names are Lukas and Andreas and they're 16 and 19. My mother is French and ⁶ _____ name is Christine. Dad is Swiss and ⁷ _____ name is Dieter. We live in Zurich and ⁸ _____ house has got four bedrooms and a small garden. We've got a dog and we think he's lovely. ⁹ _____ name's Zak.

Please tell me all about ¹⁰ _____ friends and ¹¹ _____ school in your next letter. I'd like to know about English schools.

Love,

Laura

14   Starter section

4 *have/has got*

Positive	Negative	Question	Short answer
I/you/we/they 've (have) got	I/you/we/they **haven't** (have not) got	Have I/you/we/they got ...?	Yes, I/you/we/they **have**. No, I/you/we/they **haven't** (have not).
he/she/it 's (has) got	he/she/it **hasn't** (has not) got	Has he/she/it got ...?	Yes, he/she/it **has**. No, he/she/it **hasn't** (has not).

a 🔊 Listen to the dialogue between Marek and Monica and answer the questions.

1 How many brothers and sisters has Marek got?
2 How many brothers and sisters has Monica got?

b 🔊 Listen again and complete the table.

	Age	Colour of hair	Colour of eyes
Milos	....	*fair*	....
Silvia	....	....	....
Lisa	....	....	....

c Follow the lines and write sentences with *have/has got*.

My brother hasn't got a bicycle.

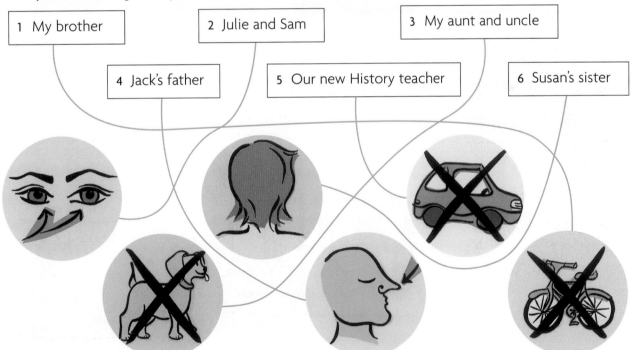

1 My brother
2 Julie and Sam
3 My aunt and uncle
4 Jack's father
5 Our new History teacher
6 Susan's sister

d Work with a partner. Ask and answer the questions. Note down your partner's answers.

1 you / any sisters and brothers?
Have you got any sisters and brothers?
2 you / a pet?
3 you / a bicycle?
4 your parents / a car?
5 your family / a flat or a house?
6 your flat *or* house / a garden?
7 (*your own question*)

e Write sentences about your partner.

Giovanna has got a brother, but she hasn't got any sisters. She's got a dog and ...

G Activities

1 Verbs for activities

Write the verbs under the pictures.

open	close	run	swim
listen	read	jump	~~laugh~~
cry	write	shout	smile

 1 *laugh*

 2 _____

 3 _____

 4 _____

 5 _____

 6 _____

 7 _____

 8 _____

 9 _____

 10 _____

11 _____

12 _____

2 Imperatives

> **Remember: imperatives**
>
> **Positive:**
> Use the base form of the verb.
> *Open* the door!
>
> **Negative:**
> Use *Don't* + the base form of the verb.
> *Don't run!*

a Match the sentences.

1 It isn't funny.
2 I want to take a photo.
3 I've got an interesting story.
4 The river is dangerous.
5 I haven't got your phone number.
6 They're my letters.

a Write it in my address book, please.
b Don't swim here.
c Don't read them.
d Smile!
e Don't laugh.
f Listen to me.

b What are the people saying? Use the imperative form of five verbs from Exercise 1.

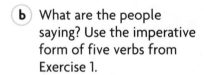

1 _____ the window!

2 I'm sorry.
_____ !

3 _____ !

4 _____ the door!

5 _____ !

3 *can/can't* **for ability**

Positive	Negative	Question	Short answer
I/you/we/they/ he/she/it **can** swim.	I/you/we/they/he/she/ it **can't** (**cannot**) swim.	**Can** I/you/we/they/ he/she/it swim?	Yes, I/you/we/they/he/she/it **can.** No, I/you/we/they/he/she/it **can't** (**cannot**).

a 🔊 Listen to Marek and Liz talking about what they can and can't do. Fill in the first two columns of the table.

✓✓ = Yes ✓ = Yes, but not very well ✗ = No

b Write sentences. Use the information from the table.

Marek can't swim. Liz can swim, but not very well.

c What about you? Fill in the column under *You* in the table.

d Work with a partner. Ask questions and fill in the last column in the table.

A: *Can you swim?*
B: *Yes, I can. Can you ...?*

	Marek	Liz	You	Your partner
1	✗			
2				
3				
4				

4 *can/can't* **for permission**

a 🔊 Listen to the dialogues and match them with the pictures. Write 1–4 in the boxes.

a
b
c
d

b 🔊 Complete the questions from Exercise 4a. Then listen again and check.

1 .... the window, please?
2 .... on these trainers, please?
3 .... it for the party, please?
4 .... an ice cream, please?

c Work with a partner. Use the pictures to make dialogues.

H Shopping for clothes

1 Clothes

1 T-shirt

2 _____

3 _____

4 _____

5 _____

6 _____

7 _____

8 _____

9 _____

10 _____

11 _____

12 _____

a Put the letters in order to make words for clothes. Match them with the pictures.

> scosk   hoses   ~~siThrt~~
> sreds   strik   hirst
> muprej   najse   scraf
> inatrers   usrtosre   tekcaj

b Say what colour the clothes are.

The T-shirt is blue.
The trainers are white.

c Work with a partner or in a small group. Ask and answer questions about clothes.

A: _What colour is your favourite shirt?_
B: _Blue. What colour are your favourite shoes?_
A: _They're ...._

2 Money and prices

a Listen to the prices and write the numbers 1–6. Then listen again and repeat.

☐ £2.50
☐ €25.00
☐ $125
☐ €17.50
☐ $11.25
☐ £15.99

Remember

We write:	We say:
£12	_twelve pounds_
€10	_ten euros_
£5.99	_five pounds ninety-nine_
€7.25	_seven euros twenty-five_
$8.60	_eight dollars sixty_

b Say the prices of the clothes in Exercise 1a.

c Work with a partner. Ask and answer.

A: _How much is the T-shirt?_
B: _It's twelve pounds. How much are the trainers?_
A: _They're ..._

Remember

To ask about prices, we say: _How much is/are ...?_

3 | *this/that/these/those*

a Match the sentences with the pictures. Write the numbers 1–4.

1 Look at this book!
2 Don't read that book. It isn't very good.
3 These books are heavy!
4 Those books are expensive.

b Complete the table.

Singular	Plural
this	....
....	those

c (Circle) the correct words.

1 (This) / These film is interesting.
2 I think *that / those* dresses are lovely.
3 *This / These* jeans are my favourite clothes.
4 *That / Those* shirt isn't very expensive.
5 *This / These* green jacket is my father's.
6 Don't open *that / those* window, please.
7 Listen to *this / these* songs.

d Complete the sentences with *this, these, that* or *those*.

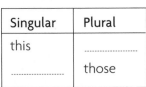
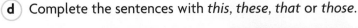

1 *Those* T-shirts are nice.

2 .... CD is really good.

3 How much is .... computer?

4 .... books are all in French!

5 .... jumper is my mother's.

6 .... pizza isn't very good.

7 .... people are Italian.

8 How much are .... trainers?

Module 1
Here and now

YOU WILL LEARN ABOUT ...

✱ Can you match each photo with a topic?

YOU WILL LEARN HOW TO ...

Speak
- Talk about your likes and dislikes
- Talk about your favourite school subjects
- Discuss household jobs
- Roleplay ordering a meal in a restaurant
- Interview a partner about food and fitness

Write
- A letter about yourself and your hobbies
- A description of your school day
- An email about organising a social event
- A paragraph about a partner's eating habits

Read
- An article about an unusual hobby
- An interview about home education
- An article about a British student's school
- An article about a volunteer worker
- Advice about healthy eating
- A menu
- Interview answers on eating habits in Britain

Listen
- Interviews about hobbies
- A dialogue about school subjects
- A radio interview about volunteer work
- A dialogue in a restaurant

Use grammar

Can you match the names of the grammar points with the examples?

Present simple
like + -ing
Object pronouns
Present continuous
Countable and uncountable nouns
much and *many*

Pauline **is staying** in Belize.
Can I have **an apple** and **some juice**, please?
She **likes swimming**.
How many eggs do you need?
Julie **wants** to be a pilot.
Sometimes our parents teach **us**.

Use vocabulary

Can you think of two more examples for each topic?

Hobbies and interests	School subjects	Housework	Food
going to the cinema	Maths	do the cooking	tomato
dancing	Geography	do the ironing	bread
....	....	....	....
....	....	....	....

Things we like doing

* Present simple (positive and negative), *like + -ing*
* Vocabulary: hobbies and interests

1 Read and listen

a Look at the picture of Julie Baker. Where do you think she comes from? What's her hobby? Read the text quickly to check your ideas.

b 🔊 Now read the text again and listen. Answer the questions.

1 How old is Julie?
2 What 'normal' activities does she like?
3 What does she learn on Sundays from 8.00 to 10.45?
4 What doesn't Julie like very much?
5 What does Julie want to be in the future?

An unusual hobby

Julie Baker is 16 and Australian. She likes music, swimming, going to the cinema and hanging out with friends. She's a very normal 16-year-old. But she has an unusual hobby: flying helicopters.

Julie is a student at the Helicopter Flying School near Brisbane. Here is her typical Sunday:

7.00	Julie gets up.
7.45–8.00	Julie's parents drive her to the helicopter school. (Julie hasn't got a driving licence.)
8.00–10.45	Her lessons start. Julie is in a group with five other students. The teacher tells them how to fly a helicopter, for example, how to take off and how to land. Julie doesn't like classroom work very much, but she knows it's important.
11.00–12.00	Julie and her friends learn how to use the radio and how to read maps.
12.00–1.00	Julie is in the pilot's seat and her teacher is next to her. She flies for one hour. She loves it. She enjoys looking down at the Sunshine Coast.
1.15	Julie's dad drives her home. He's very happy that she's back and that she's OK. 'I hate watching Julie up in that helicopter,' he says. 'Her mother and I get nervous. But we know she loves flying. She wants to be a pilot and we don't want to stop her.'

2 Grammar

Present simple (positive and negative)

a Look at the examples.
Then complete the rule.

*Her lessons **start** at 8 o'clock.*
*I **hate** watching Julie in the helicopter.*
*Julie **gets** up at 7 o'clock.*
*She **likes** music.*

> **Rule:** We use the present simple for things which happen regularly or which are always true.
>
> With *I*, _____ , *we* and _____ we use the base form of the verb. With *he, she* and *it* we add _____ .

Look

With *he, she* and *it*, some verbs end in *es*.

-*sh*   they wash – she wash**es**
-*ch*   we teach – he teach**es**,
        I watch – she watch**es**

If the verb ends with consonant + *y*, the ending is *ies*.
they fly – it fl**ies**
you study – he stud**ies**

b Complete the sentences.
Use the present simple form of the verbs.

1   Cristina ___loves___ (love) parties.
2   My friends _____ (hate) sport.
3   You _____ (paint) nice pictures.
4   He _____ (write) his emails on my computer.
5   Pete and Sandra _____ (play) tennis on Mondays.
6   My mum _____ (read) a lot of books.
7   We _____ (get up) at 8.30 in the morning.

c Write present simple sentences.
Use *like, love* or *hate* and a word from the box.

| cats   football   ~~apples~~   ice cream   bananas   winter |

1   He ___likes apples___ .   2   I _____ .

3   She _____ .   4   They _____ .

5   He _____ .   6   We _____ .

d Look at the examples and complete the table.

*Julie **doesn't like** classroom work.*
*We **don't want** to stop her.*

Positive	Negative
I/you/we/they **run**	I/you/we/they _____ (**do not**) run
he/she/it **runs**	he/she/it _____ (**does not**) run

e Make the sentences negative.

1   Tracy likes black jeans. ___Tracy doesn't like black jeans.___
2   We write lots of emails. _____
3   My brother plays the piano. _____
4   Helen learns Italian at school. _____
5   You listen to the teacher. _____

f Complete the sentences. Use the verbs in the box in the present simple (positive or negative).

| fly | run | ~~hate~~ | not drive | not know | not swim |

1 I ___hate___ this music!

2 We _____ in this river.

3 Jamie _____ to Rome in the summer.

4 Bill's parents _____ a big car.

5 Teresa _____ the answer.

6 Lesley _____ in the park before school.

3 Vocabulary

Hobbies and interests

a 🔊 Match the activities with the pictures. Write 1–8 in the boxes. Then listen, check and repeat.

1 going to the cinema
2 reading
3 swimming
4 painting
5 playing computer games
6 dancing
7 listening to music
8 playing the guitar

b Match words from the three lists to make five true sentences.

	play	
	plays	
	don't play	a lot of books.
	listen	the piano.
I	go	at parties.
My friend	goes	to pop music.
My brother	read	computer games.
My sister	don't read	football.
	doesn't read	to the cinema.
	dance	
	doesn't dance	

4 Grammar

like + -ing

a Look at the examples and complete the rule.

*She likes **swimming**.* *She enjoys **looking** down at the coast.*
*She loves **flying**.* *I hate **watching** Julie in that helicopter.*

> **Rule:** We often use the *-ing* form after verbs of liking and not liking, for example, *like*, ... , ...
> and ....

Look

If the verb ends in *e*, we drop the *e* before *-ing*.
dance – dancing, smile – smiling

If a short verb ends in vowel + consonant, we double the last letter before *-ing*.
swim – swi**mm**ing, run – ru**nn**ing

b Complete the sentences. Use the *-ing* form of the verbs in the box.

> drive run ~~play~~ go listen talk

1 Maria hates ___*playing*___ the piano.
2 My brother loves .... his car.
3 I like .... to my friends on the phone.
4 My dad doesn't like .... to loud music.
5 Our dogs enjoy .... on the beach.
6 We love .... to the cinema.

5 Speak

Work with a partner. Talk about the hobbies in Exercise 3.
Note down the things your partner tells you.

I love ... I (don't) like/enjoy ... I hate ... I'm (not) good at ...

6 Listen

a 🔊 Listen to Kate, Adrian and Harry. Write ✓ next to the things they like and ✗ next to the things they don't like.

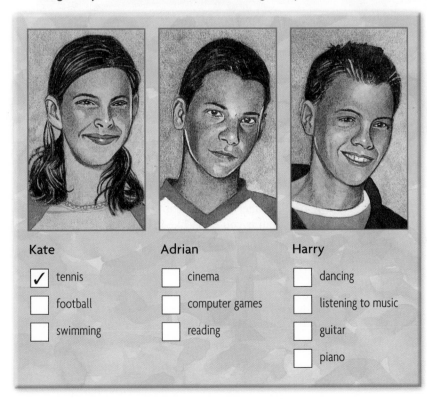

Kate
- ✓ tennis
- ☐ football
- ☐ swimming

Adrian
- ☐ cinema
- ☐ computer games
- ☐ reading

Harry
- ☐ dancing
- ☐ listening to music
- ☐ guitar
- ☐ piano

b Work with a partner. Talk about the three teenagers and check your answers.

A: *What's Kate's hobby?*
B: *She likes ..., but she doesn't like ...*

7 Pronunciation

/n/ (*ma**n***) and /ŋ/ (*so**ng***)

a 🔊 Listen and repeat.

| /n/ | man fun town Japan Britain Italian |
| /ŋ/ | thing song spring morning writing reading |

b 🔊 Listen and repeat.

Karen likes dancing and painting.
Dan enjoys running in the morning.
We sing songs at the station.

Different – so what?

8 Read and listen

(a) 🔊 Look at the photo story. Who is 'different' in the story, and why? Read and listen to find the answers.

1

Alex: Look at that guy over there.
Dave: What about him?
Alex: That's Tony Smith.

2

Dave: Oh, Tony. That's right. He goes to ballet classes.
Alex: Yeah, that's weird! A boy! Doing ballet!

3

Dave: Hey, Tony. Do you want to play football with us?
Alex: Or are you worried about your pretty little dancing feet?
Dave: Alex, shut up! Don't listen to him, Tony, he's stupid.

4

Tony: You know, Alex, I like playing football. And, no, I'm not worried about my feet.
Alex: Oh, yeah? But doing ballet ...

5

Tony: I like ballet. It's my hobby. It's not my problem if you don't like it!
Alex: Well, I mean, it's different, isn't it? For a boy ...
Tony: So what?

(b) Write the correct name, *Tony*, *Dave* or *Alex*.

1 .... goes to ballet classes.
2 .... thinks ballet is only for girls.
3 .... asks Tony to play football.
4 .... is angry with Alex.
5 .... doesn't care what Alex thinks.

(c) What do you think about what Alex says to Tony?

9 Everyday English

(a) Find expressions 1–5 in the photo story. Who says them?
Match them with expressions a–e.

1 guy
2 What about him?
3 That's weird!
4 Shut up!
5 So what?

a Be quiet!
b I don't think it's important.
c teenage boy or man
d very strange
e What do you want to say about him?

(b) Read the dialogues.
Fill in the spaces with the
underlined words in Exercise 9a.

1 Linda: _Shut up_ , Peter!
   You say really stupid things.
   Peter: OK, sorry. Don't be
   angry.

2 Susan: Do you know Ken
   Taylor?
   Karen: Yes. He's in my class.
   He's a nice ....

3 Rob: Our dog likes sleeping
   in the bath.
   Judith: That's .... !

4 Tom: You like playing football?
   But you're a girl!
   Gina: .... ? Why can't
   a girl play football?

5 Mike: Is that Claire, the new
   girl in your class?
   Monica: Yes. .... her?
   Mike: I think she's John
   Cooper's sister.

10 Write

(a) Imagine that Lisa is your new penfriend and this is her
first letter to you. Read her letter. What are her hobbies
and interests?

> Hi!
>
> I'm Lisa Franklin. I'm Canadian and
> I live in Montreal. I'm fifteen.
>
> I love sports. My favourite hobby is
> painting. I also like playing tennis
> (I'm in a tennis club at school) and
> I enjoy riding my bike. I love watching
> TV, especially Formula 1 races! I really
> like Michael Schumacher.
>
> My best friend is Sonia. We listen
> to music a lot. Her favourite singer
> is Alanis Morissette. I think Alanis
> is a great singer, but my favourite is
> Jennifer Lopez.
>
> Write soon!
>
> Lisa

(b) Write a letter in reply to Lisa. Include this information:

- your name, nationality and age
- where you live
- your hobbies and interests
- some information about your friend(s)

For your portfolio

2 School life

✱ Present simple (questions and short answers), object pronouns
✱ Vocabulary: school subjects, frequency expressions

1 Read and listen

a Where is Matthew and how does he study? Does he enjoy it? Read the text quickly to find the answers.

b 🔊 Now read the text again and listen. Answer the questions.

1 How old is Matthew?
2 Why doesn't he go to school?
3 What subjects does Matthew study?
4 Why does he like studying at home?
5 Why doesn't Matthew get lonely?
6 Where does he see his friends?

c What do you think are the good things about learning at home, and what are the bad things? Make two lists and compare with your partner.

AT HOME –
AT SCHOOL

Bolivia
Arica ○
Chile
Pacific Ocean
Argentina

Matthew Thomas is English. He is 15 and his brother Paul is 13, but they don't go to school. They are in the Chilean city of Arica for a year because their parents are scientists there. They study at home. Here is our interview with Matthew about home education.

Why do you study at home?

M: Well, there aren't any English-speaking schools here and we don't speak very good Spanish. And we think you can learn a lot at home.

What subjects do you study?

M: The usual subjects – Maths, English, History, and so on. But I study them in my own way. I use books or the Internet. And sometimes our parents teach us.

Do you like studying at home?

M: Yes, I do – I love it! I can choose how to do things. I can study Maths on Monday and Physics on Tuesday, or Biology on Monday and History on Tuesday. It's up to me.

Does your brother like it, too?

M: Yes, he does. I often help him – and sometimes he helps me.

Do you get lonely?

M: No, I don't. I'm hardly ever lonely. My brother and my parents are here. I've got friends on the Internet and now I've got a few Chilean friends, too.

How often do you see them?

M: Well, I go to a sports club every weekend and I meet them there. And I go to a dance club twice a month. That's always good fun.

2 Grammar

Present simple
(questions and short answers)

(a) Read the examples and complete the table.

Do you *like* studying at home?   Yes, I *do*.
Does your brother *like* it, too?   Yes, he *does*.
Do you *get* lonely?   No, I *don't*.

Questions	Short answers
.... I/you/ we/they like *...ing?*	Yes, I/you/we/they **do**. No, I/you/we/they .... (**do not**).
.... he/ she/it like *...ing?*	Yes, he/she/it .... No, he/she/it **doesn't** (............... **not**).

(b) Complete the questions and short answers.

1 A: *Does* Jeremy like swimming?
   B: (✓) *Yes, he does* .
2 A: .... you study French?
   B: (✗) *No, I* ....
3 A: .... your friends listen to music?
   B: (✓) *Yes,* ....
4 A: .... she go to your school?
   B: (✓) ....
5 A: .... you wear a uniform to school?
   B: (✗) ....
6 A: .... it rain a lot in Britain?
   B: (✓) ....

(c) Work with a partner. Ask and answer.

A: *Do you like swimming?*
B: *Yes, I do. / No, I don't. Do you ...?*

live   eat   go   play   ~~walk~~   drive

1 ...*Do*... you ...*like*... ...*walking*... to school?
2 .... you .... chocolate?
3 .... your family .... in a flat?
4 .... your friends .... to the cinema?
5 .... your mother .... a car?
6 .... you .... the piano?

3 Vocabulary

School subjects

(a) 🔊 Write the subjects under the pictures. Then listen, check and repeat.

Maths   English   Science   Art   French
Information Technology (IT)   History
~~Geography~~   Physical Education (PE)   Drama

1 *Geography* ....   2 ....

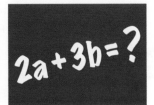

3 ....   4 ....

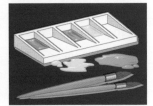

5 ....   6 ....

7 ....   8 ....

9 ....   10 ....

(b) Are there any subjects at your school which are not in Exercise 3a? What are they?

(c) Make a list of your five favourite subjects. Compare lists with a partner.

4 Grammar

Object pronouns

a Look at the examples from the text on page 28 and fill in the spaces.

I love **it**.	'it'	=	_studying at home_
I study **them** in my own way.	'them'	=	....
Sometimes our parents teach **us**.	'us'	=	....
I often help **him**	'him'	=	....
and sometimes he helps **me**.	'me'	=	....

b Write the object pronouns in the spaces.

I ___me___ you .... he .... she .... it .... we .... they ....

c Complete the sentences with object pronouns.

1 This is a great CD! I really like ___it___ .
2 Who's that boy? I don't know ....
3 This exercise is difficult! Can you help .... , please?
4 Where are my shoes? I can't find ....
5 We don't know the answer. Can you tell .... ?
6 Mariah is a great singer. I like .... a lot.
7 Good morning. Can I help .... ?

5 Vocabulary

Adverbs of frequency

a Look at the diagram and complete the sentences about Matthew. Check with the text on page 28.

100% ◄─────────────────────────► 0%
always   usually   often   sometimes   hardly ever   never

1 Matthew ___never___ goes to school.
2 He .... has fun when he goes to the dance club.
3 He .... helps his brother with his studies.
4 His parents .... teach him at home.
5 He's .... lonely.

b Complete the rule. Write *before* or *after*.

> **Rule:** Adverbs of frequency come .... the verb *be*, but .... other verbs.

c Put the adverbs in the sentences.

1 I'm late. (always) _I'm always late._
2 We go to the cinema. (sometimes)
   ....
3 Carlo goes to bed early. (hardly ever)
   ....
4 Those dogs are quiet! (never)
   ....
5 Elizabeth listens to music. (often)
   ....
6 You're good at Maths. (usually)
   ....

d We can also talk about frequency like this:

every		day
once		week
twice	a	month
three times		year

*I go to a sports club **every week**.*
*I go to a dance club **twice a month**.*
*We study History **three times a week**.*

How often do you ...

1 go to school?   3 have exams?
2 have Science lessons?   4 play sport?

6 Pronunciation

Stress in frequency expressions

a 🔊 Listen and repeat.

sometimes	usually
always	hardly ever
every weekend	once a month
twice a day	three times a week
	twenty times a year

b 🔊 Underline the main stress. Then listen and repeat again.

7 Speak

Work with a partner. Ask and answer questions and note down your partner's answers.

- go to the cinema?
- watch television?
- drink coffee?
- use a computer?
- cook at home?
- eat chocolate?
- see your best friend?
- go swimming?
- (your ideas)

A: *How often do you go to the cinema?*
B: *Every weekend. / Once a month.*

8 Listen

a 🔊 Listen to Jane talking about her school timetable. Complete the timetable. Write: *PE, IT, Drama, Art* and *English*.

	Monday	Tuesday	Wednesday	Thursday	Friday
8.45–9.45	1	History	English	Geography	English
9.45–10.45	IT	French	IT	French	2
10.45–11.00	*Break*				
11.00–12.00	Maths	Geography	History	Maths	Maths
12.00–1.00	PE	3	4	5	Science
1.00–2.00	*Lunch break*				
2.00–3.00	Science	6	Maths	Science	French
3.00–4.30	*Games / clubs*				

b 🔊 Listen again. Write ✓ for the subjects Jane likes, and ✗ for the ones she doesn't like.

PE	☐	IT	☐
Drama	☐	Art	☐

c Work with a partner. Compare Jane's timetable with your school timetable. For example:

She studies French, but we study German. She has Maths four times a week, but we have it five times a week.

Culture in mind

9 Read

a Alan Martin is 16 and he's in year 11 at a British school. Read the text quickly to answer the questions.

1 When does school start and finish?

2 What does Alan do after school?

b Read again. Match the topics with the paragraphs in the text. Write 1–6 in the boxes.

a Activities after school ☐

b Free time between lessons ☐

c School clothes ☐

d School subjects in year 11 ☐

e Homework ☐

f The start of the school day ☐

c Circle the correct words.

1 He *wears* / *doesn't wear* a uniform at the weekend.

2 There is a school Assembly on Monday *mornings* / *afternoons*.

3 Brian *likes* / *doesn't like* learning languages.

4 Alan's friends *sometimes* / *never* bring sandwiches to school.

5 Alan goes to clubs *once* / *twice* a week.

6 He *does* / *doesn't do* a lot of homework.

d Answer the questions.

1 Do girls go to Alan's school?

2 Do all British students wear a uniform?

3 Does Alan go to school by bus?

4 How many subjects does Alan study?

5 Where does he eat his lunch?

6 How many hours a week does Alan spend on homework?

e Is Alan's school day similar to yours, or very different? Discuss this question with a partner or in a small group.

A school in Britain

1 I get up at 7.30 and get dressed for school. My school has a uniform – black trousers and shoes, a white shirt and a black and gold tie. The girls wear the same, or they can wear a black skirt. We also have a black sweatshirt or we can wear a black jacket. Not all British schools have a uniform, but it's common here.

2 I don't live far from the school, so I walk there with my friends, Brian and Gemma. Lots of students catch the school bus or their parents drive them to school. On Mondays we all start the day with Assembly in the school hall at 8.50. The headteacher talks to us and gives us information about school events.

3 This year I've got nine subjects. We all study English, Maths and Science, and then we choose other subjects. My favourites are IT and Art & Design. Brian likes Spanish and Japanese. Gemma is brilliant at Maths, so she goes to an Advanced Maths class.

4 We have 20 minutes for break in the morning and an hour for lunch. Some students bring sandwiches to school for lunch, but my friends and I always eat in the dining room where you can get a hot meal every day.

5 Lessons end at 4 o'clock, but on Mondays and Wednesdays I stay at school until 5 o'clock. I go to the Photography Club and the Athletics Club. There are lots of clubs and activities at our school. Brian belongs to the Film Society and Gemma plays in the school orchestra.

6 At the end of the day I always spend two hours on homework – sometimes three hours. We get lots of homework now. We've got our GCSE* exams in June, so there's always *lots* of work to do.

*GCSE = national school exams (General Certificate of Secondary Education). Students usually take these examinations when they are 16.

10 Write

(a) Answer the questions.

1 What time do you usually get up?
2 What time do you leave your home?
3 What time do the lessons begin?
4 What time do you have a break?
5 Do you have lunch at school? What do you eat?
6 What time do the lessons finish?
7 What do you do after school?
8 How much time do you spend on homework in the evening?

(b) Write a description of your usual school day. Use your answers in Exercise 10a to help you.

For your portfolio

3 A helping hand

* Present continuous for activities happening now, Present simple vs. present continuous
* Vocabulary: housework

1 Read and listen

(a) How old is Pauline? Where is she and what is she doing there? Read the text quickly to find the answers.

(b) 🔊 Now read the text again and listen. Mark the statements *T* (true) or *F* (false).

1 Pauline comes from Belize. ☐

2 Pauline wants to save the coral reefs. ☐

3 Pauline is studying the fish in the sea near Belize. ☐

4 Pauline is unhappy because she doesn't get any money. ☐

5 Pauline wants to go home when she finishes her work. ☐

(c) Answer the questions.

1 Why does Pauline like the work she's doing?

2 Would you like to work as a volunteer in another part of the world? Why / Why not?

HARD WORK and no money

Every year thousands of young people in Britain finish school and then take a year off before they start work or go to university. Some young people go to other countries and work as volunteers. Volunteers give their time to help people – for example, they work in schools or hospitals, or they help with conservation.

Pauline Jones, 18, lives in Cardiff, Wales. Next year she wants to go to university to study Spanish, but now she's living in Belize. Pauline says, 'I'm working with other people here to protect the coral reefs in the sea near Belize. The reefs here are beautiful, but if the sea water is very polluted, the coral dies. I'm helping to do research on the coral and the fish that live around the reefs. All over the world, coral reefs are dying. We need to do something about the problem before it's too late.

I'm staying with a family here and I help with the cooking and the cleaning. I don't get any money, but that's OK. I love my work here, and I'm learning a lot about the people of Belize – and myself! When I finish my work, I want to stay here for another three months. I want to travel around Belize and Central America.'

MEXICO

BELIZE

GUATEMALA

CARIBBEAN SEA

2 Grammar

Present continuous for activities happening now

a Read the examples and the rule for the present continuous. Then complete the table.

*Pauline **is working** in Belize.*
*She's **staying** with a family.*
*The volunteers **are helping** to protect the reefs.*

> **Rule:** We use the present continuous to talk about things that are happening at or around the time of speaking.
>
> We form the present continuous with the present tense of *be* + verb + *ing*.

Positive	Negative	Questions	Short answers
I'm (am) working	I'm **not** working	.... I working?	Yes, I **am**. No, I'm **not**.
you/we/they 're (...............) working	you/we/they **aren't** working	.... you/we/they working?	Yes, you/we/they .... No, you/we/they ....
he/she/it 's (is) working	he/she/it .... working	.... he/she/it working?	Yes, he/she/it .... No, he/she/it ....

b Complete the sentences. Use the present continuous form of the verbs.

1 Anna isn't here. She *'s riding* (ride) her bike in the park.
2 Mike and Jane are in the living room. They .... (read).
3 Dad's in the kitchen. He .... (cook) lunch.
4 Alan! You .... (not listen) to me!
5 I can't go out tonight. I .... (study) for tomorrow's test.
6 It's 3–0! We .... (not play) very well.
7 **A:** .... you .... (watch) this programme?
   B: No, I'm not.
8 **A:** Sandra's in her room.
   B: .... she .... (do) her homework?

c Look at the pictures and complete the sentences. Use the verbs in the box.

> listen   play   write   not work
> not do   not watch

1 My grandfather .... a letter.
2 Rosa .... television.
3 Marcia and Louise .... to music.
4 I .... my homework.
5 We .... a fantastic computer game.
6 My parents .... in the garden.

3 Pronunciation /ɜː/ (w_orld)

a 🔊 Listen and repeat the words.

her world work learn b_ir_thday univ_er_sity

b 🔊 Listen and repeat the sentences.

1 All over the world.
2 He always works hard.
3 Learn these words!
4 They weren't at university.
5 I'm learning German.
6 This is her first birthday.

Look

These verbs are hardly ever used in the present continuous:

believe know understand remember want need mean like hate

I **know** the answer.
(Not: ~~I'm knowing~~ the answer.)

My friend **likes** rap music.
(Not: ~~My friend is liking~~ rap music.)

4 Grammar

Present simple vs. present continuous

a Look at the examples. Then (circle) the correct words in the sentences.

Present simple	Present continuous
It sometimes **snows** *in the winter.*	*It's* **snowing** *now.*
My mother **works** *in a bank.*	*She's* **working** *in the kitchen at the moment.*
They **play** *tennis every Saturday.*	*They aren't here. They're* **playing** *tennis this morning.*

1 *We always wear / We're always wearing* a uniform to school.
2 Paula *wears / is wearing* black jeans today.
3 Come inside! *It rains / It's raining.*
4 *It rains / It's raining* a lot in February.
5 Mum *cooks / is cooking* at the moment.
6 My father *cooks / is cooking* lunch every Sunday.
7 Steve is terrible! *He never listens / He's never listening* to the teacher!
8 Please be quiet! *I listen / I'm listening* to some music right now.

b We use different time expressions with the two tenses. Complete the lists with the time expressions in the box.

at the moment	usually	every weekend
this afternoon	never	right now	today
every evening	this week	twice a year

Present simple	Present continuous
every day	*now*
always	*this morning*
....	....
....	....
....	....
....	....

c Complete the sentences. Use the present simple or present continuous form of the verbs.

①    ②

③    ④

⑤    ⑥

1 Maria usually .... (walk) to school, but this week she .... (go) by bus.
2 We .... (have) English lessons four times a week. We .... (read) Shakespeare at the moment.
3 Robert .... (study) in the library this afternoon. He .... (want) to find some information for his History project.
4 I .... (know) her face, but I .... (not remember) her name.
5 They .... (not dance) tonight because they .... (not like) the music.
6 What .... this word .... (mean)?

5 Listen

a 🔊 Listen to a radio interview with Pauline Jones. What is Pauline doing at the time of the interview? Choose the correct picture.

a

b

c

b 🔊 Listen again and mark the sentences *T* (true) or *F* (false).

1   Pauline doesn't have a lot of free time. ☐

2   She sometimes does the cooking. ☐

3   She does the shopping every day. ☐

4   She likes doing the washing. ☐

5   She's happy to be in Belize. ☐

6 Vocabulary

Housework

🔊 Match the words with the pictures. Then listen, check and repeat.

1 do the cooking   2 do the ironing   3 do the washing
4 do the shopping   5 do the washing-up / wash up
6 tidy up / tidy a room   7 clean the windows

Look

do the washing-up / wash up = wash dishes

do the washing = wash clothes

7 Speak

a Work in a group. Ask and answer questions about housework.

Do you help at home?
How often do you do the shopping / the washing-up ...?
Which jobs do you like? Which do you hate?

b In your home, who usually does the housework? You? Your brother or sister? Your mother? Your father? Discuss with a partner.

My father usually does the cooking, but my mother always does the washing-up ...

Where's Amy going?

8 Read and listen

a 🔊 Look at the photo story. Why can't Amy go to the café?
Read, listen and check your answer.

1 Amy: OK. Good. Two o'clock. See you then. Bye.

2 Alex: Hi, Amy. That new café is open today. We're going there now to check it out. Do you want to come?
Amy: Um ... sorry, no. I'd like to, but I'm busy.

3 Alex: Strange. Why doesn't she want to come?
Dave: I know! Maybe she's got a boyfriend.

4 *Half an hour later ...*
Alex: Look, there's Amy. Where's she going?
Dave: I think she's got a boyfriend. Let's follow her.

5 Amy: Here's your shopping, Mrs Craig. Do you want me to do the ironing too?
Mrs Craig: Thanks very much, Amy. You're an angel.

Alex: So it's not a boyfriend. She's doing jobs for Mrs Craig.
Dave: She must be crazy!

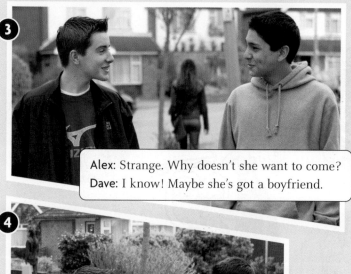

b Match the two parts of the sentences.

1	Alex and Dave are going	a	she's busy.
2	Amy says she can't come because	b	she's got a boyfriend.
3	Dave thinks that	c	is helping an old person.
4	They follow Amy and find out that	d	to the new café.
5	Dave can't understand why Amy	e	she's helping Mrs Craig.

9 Everyday English

(a) Find the expressions in the photo story. Who says them?

1 We're going there now to check it out.
2 You're an angel.
3 She must be crazy!
4 Let's follow her.

(b) How do you say *Let's follow her* in your language?

(c) Match expressions 1–3 from the photo story with expressions a–c.

1 <u>check it out</u>
2 <u>You're an angel.</u>
3 <u>She must be crazy.</u>

a You're a really nice person.
b find out what it's like
c I can't understand her.

(d) Read the dialogues. Fill in the spaces with the <u>underlined</u> expressions from Exercises 9b and 9c.

1 **Tom:** Mum wants to buy a new computer.
  Sarah: .... She's already got a very good computer.

2 **Rick:** Adam says the music is good at the Starlight Disco.
  Mike: Yeah. I'd like to .... soon.

3 **Franca:** Do you want to go out this evening?
  Martina: Yes, ... go to the cinema.

4 **Paul:** I'm going to clean the windows for you, Gran.
  Grandmother: Oh, thanks, Paul. ....

10 Write

(a) Read Peter's email to his friend about a family party. Answer the questions.

1 What is the event and when is it happening?
2 Who is coming?
3 What is everybody doing to help?

Get Msg Write Msg Reply File Delete Stop Print

Hi Richard!

This is just a quick message, because I'm really busy. We're all getting ready for my grandfather's sixtieth birthday. There's a big family party this evening in the garden, with about 40 people.
So this afternoon we're cleaning and tidying up. My mother is cooking in the kitchen and my aunts are helping her. Dad is putting up lights in the garden at the moment, and my uncle is organising the tables and chairs. My cousins are here too, but they aren't helping much – they're playing computer games.

I must go now. See you on Monday.

Peter

(b) Imagine you are helping to prepare for one of these events:

- a family party
- a birthday celebration for one of your friends
- a goodbye party for a teacher who is leaving the school

Write an email to a friend and tell him/her what is happening.

For your portfolio

4 A healthy life

❋ Countable and uncountable nouns, *a/an* and *some*, *much* and *many*
❋ Vocabulary: food and drink

1 Read and listen

(a) Before you read, look at the questions and choose the answers you think are correct. Then read the text to check your answers.

1 What nationality are the people in the photo?
 a Chinese **b** Japanese **c** Russian

2 How many meals do you need every day?
 a one **b** three **c** five

3 Is it a good idea to eat snacks?
 a yes **b** no **c** it doesn't matter

4 How often do you need to exercise?
 a every day **b** once a week **c** three times a week

Getting **fat** or keeping fit?

Some people want to get fat – Japanese Sumo wrestlers, for example. Their typical meal is called *chankonabe*, a mixture of rice, meat and vegetables. It's healthy, but it has a lot of calories.

It's difficult to throw a very heavy man to the floor! This is why Sumo wrestlers eat a lot of food and go to bed straight after eating. Some Sumo wrestlers weigh 250 kilograms, a few of them even 280 kilograms!

But most people want to keep their weight down. In Britain and the USA, doctors are worried that a lot of teenagers are overweight.

They often eat unhealthy food and spend a lot of time sitting in front of the television or the computer.

Here's some advice:

- Have some vegetables or some fruit in every meal. Tomatoes are great!

- Eat five small meals a day instead of two or three large meals.

- It's a good idea to eat snacks, but don't eat a lot of sugar. Have some bread, an apple, some grapes or a carrot.

- Don't eat fried food very often. Have some rice or some pasta instead.

- Drink a lot of water. If you want a sweet drink, have some fruit juice.

- Do some exercise every day. Exercise burns off the calories and makes you fit. So come on – get up and ride your bike, swim, run, go for walks!

- Finally, remember – there's no need to be skinny! Enjoy your food and have fun when you're exercising.

(b) 🔊 Now read the text again and listen. Answer the questions.

1 What kind of food do Sumo wrestlers usually eat? Why?
2 Why do you think Sumo wrestlers go to bed straight after their dinner?
3 Why are many teenagers in the UK and USA overweight?
4 Do you agree with all the advice in the text? If not, why?

2 Vocabulary

Food and drink

🔊 Label the pictures. Use the words in the box. Then listen, check and repeat.

apples   carrots   eggs   meat   ~~fruit~~   bread   ~~vegetables~~   tomatoes   pasta   water   onions   sugar   grapes   rice

1 _vegetables_

2 _fruit_

3 _____

4 _____

5 _____

6 _____

7 _____

8 _____

9 _____

10 _____

11 _____

12 _____

13 _____

14 _____

3 Grammar

Countable and uncountable nouns

a Read the rule. Then <u>underline</u> the countable nouns and ⟨circle⟩ the uncountable nouns in examples 1–5.

1 Have some ⟨bread.⟩
2 Eat five small meals.
3 Don't eat fried food.
4 Have some bread, an apple, some grapes or a carrot.
5 Eat some vegetables or some fruit.

b Complete the lists with words from Exercise 2.

Countable nouns	Uncountable nouns
vegetables	fruit

Rule: In English, we can count some nouns: *1 apple, 2 bananas, 3 carrots*, etc. We call these words *countable nouns*.

There are some nouns we can't count, for example: *food* and *fruit*. These nouns have no plural. We call them *uncountable nouns*.

a/an and *some*

c Look again at the examples in Exercise 3a. Complete the rule with *countable* or *uncountable*.

Rule: We use *a/an* with singular _countable_ nouns. We use *some* with plural _____ nouns. We use *some* with singular _____ nouns.

d Complete the sentences with *a*, *an* or *some*.

1 I'd like _____ sugar in my coffee.
2 I'm going to the shops. Mum wants _____ meat and _____ eggs.
3 This is _____ lovely apple!
4 _____ onion is _____ vegetable.
5 Have _____ fruit. There are _____ nice grapes in the kitchen.
6 She needs _____ bread and _____ tomato to make a sandwich.

much and many

(e) Look at the examples. Then complete the rule.

How many meals do you have every day?
*How much water do you drink?   We haven't got **much coffee**.*
*There aren't **many vegetables** in the garden.*

(f) (Circle) the correct words in questions 1–6. Then match the questions with the answers.

1   Is there *much / many* milk in the fridge?
2   How *much / many* potatoes do you want?
3   How *much / many* time have we got?
4   Are there *much / many* people in the café?
5   How *much / many* subjects do you study?
6   How *much / many* money have you got?

a   Yes, there are about 50.
b   €15.
c   No, there isn't.
d   Two, please.
e   Ten minutes.
f   Nine.

4 Speak

(a) Work with a partner. Discuss the quiz questions and choose the answers you think are correct.

(b) Ask your partner about the things in the quiz. For example:

Do you eat a lot of hamburgers?
How many hamburgers do you eat every month?
How often do you eat an apple?

5 Pronunciation The schwa /ə/ (wat<u>er</u>)

(a) 🔊 The most common vowel sound in English is /ə/. Listen to the words and repeat.

wat<u>er</u>   sugar
tomato   b<u>a</u>nana
ex<u>er</u>cise   vegetab<u>le</u>

(b) 🔊 Listen and <u>underline</u> the syllables with the /ə/ sound. Then listen again and repeat.

<u>a</u> carr<u>ot</u>   an orange

some bread   some apples
some onions

a lot   a lot of fruit
a lot of calories
a lot of vegetables

Health Quiz

1 How many calories are there in an average hamburger?

  a 150   b 220   c 280

4 How many calories do you burn if you run for 20 minutes?

  a 200   b 300   c 400

2 How many calories are there in an apple?

  a 80   b 100   c 120

5 How much water should people drink every day?

  a half a litre   b 1 litre
  c 2–3 litres

3 How many calories do you burn if you swim for 20 minutes?

  a 60   b 90   c 140

6 How much sleep does an average person get every night?

  a 7 hours   b 8.5 hours
  c 9.5 hours

6 Listen

a 🔊 Match the dishes on the menu with the pictures. Write the numbers 1–11. Then listen and check.

a  ☐

b  ☐

c  1

d  ☐

e  ☐

f  ☐

g  ☐

h 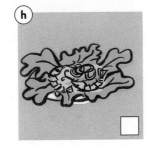 ☐

i  ☐

j  ☐

k 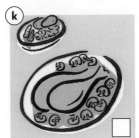 ☐

Black Horse Café

STARTERS

1	Pasta *(with fresh tomato sauce)*	£ 4.50
2	Vegetable soup	£ 2.80
3	Seafood salad	£ 5.80

MAIN MEALS

(with vegetables or salad)

4	Fish of the day (grilled or fried)	£ 8.40
5	Chicken and mushrooms	£ 7.60
6	Beefburgers	£ 6.50
7	Vegetable curry and rice	£ 6.50

ALL DRINKS — £ 1.50

8	Coffee
9	Tea
10	Mineral water
11	Orange juice

b 🔊 Listen to the dialogue at the Black Horse Café. Fill in the words from the menu.

Waiter: Are you ready to order?

Diana: Yes, I'd like to start with the soup, please, and then the grilled ¹............... .

Waiter: Certainly. Would you like vegetables or salad?

Diana: ²............... , please.

Waiter: And to drink?

Diana: I'd like an orange ³............... , I think.

Waiter: Orange juice. Fine.

Mike: And I'd like the ⁴............... salad, please. And then the ⁵............... with vegetables.

Waiter: Chicken with vegetables. And to drink?

Mike: Just some mineral ⁶............... , please.

Waiter: Right. Anything else?

Mike: No, thank you.

7 Speak

Work in a group of three. One of you is the waiter. The other two order a meal from the menu.

Culture in mind

8 Read

a) Look at photos 1–4. Can you find these things?

> some cereal bacon and eggs restaurant food an omelette
> some toast a sandwich a take-away fish and chips

b) Match the things in Exercise 8a with the headings from an article on British food.

1 Breakfast 2 Lunch 3 Eating out

Read the text quickly to check your answers.

What *is* British food?

When someone says 'typical British food', most people think of fish and chips, roast beef on Sundays, and bacon and eggs for breakfast. But is this what people usually eat? What do the teenagers of Britain eat today? We asked James (15), Sophie (15) and Marcus (16).

Breakfast

James: Breakfast for me is a bowl of cereal and some fruit juice. That's all.

Sophie: I never eat a big breakfast. I just have tea and a piece of toast.

Marcus: I love bacon and eggs at the weekend, but not on school days. It's too much.

Lunch

James: It depends. At school I have sandwiches. At the weekend I often have pizza or fish and chips – something quick and easy.

Sophie: I have lunch at school. It's usually some kind of meat with vegetables. At the weekend or in the holidays, I like making salads and omelettes for lunch.

Marcus: I usually just eat some fruit and perhaps a sandwich and some yoghurt. That's enough for me.

(c) **Read again and answer the questions.**

1 What is a typical British Sunday dish?
2 Does Sophie eat a lot for breakfast?
3 When does Marcus have bacon and eggs for breakfast?
4 Who likes an egg dish for lunch?
5 Why doesn't James eat out very often?
6 Where does Marcus sometimes eat out?

(d) **What are the main differences between your eating habits and those of James, Sophie and Marcus?**

Eating out

James: I live in a very small town and there aren't many restaurants here. But I like Chinese food a lot and we often get a Chinese take-away. My parents sometimes take us out to a restaurant – then it's usually French or Italian food.

Sophie: Indian dishes are my favourite food. There are some really good Indian restaurants here, and I often go to one with my friends. I love chicken tikka masala. Actually, that's one of the most popular dishes in Britain these days.

Marcus: I'm lucky – I live in London and you can get anything here. I don't eat out very often, but I like Greek food so I sometimes go to a Greek restaurant.

9 Write

(a) **Write notes in answer to these questions.**

1 How many meals do you eat every day?
2 What food do you often eat? What don't you eat?
3 Do you eat healthy snacks?
4 How much water do you drink a day?
5 What do you do to keep fit?

(b) **Work with a partner. Ask and answer the questions and note down your partner's answers.**

(c) **Write a paragraph about your partner. Use your notes to guide you. Here is an example.**

Carol eats three meals a day. She eats a lot of salad and vegetables, but not much meat. She hates carrots! She doesn't eat a lot of snacks but she sometimes has an ice cream or some chocolate. She drinks two litres of water a day. Keeping fit is very important for Carol. She plays basketball once a week. She also swims and rides her bike, and she enjoys going for walks at the weekend.

For your portfolio

1 **Grammar**

a Complete the sentences with object pronouns.

1 I really like you. Do you like ___me___ ?

2 She's in my class, but I don't know _____ very well.

3 Dad! Alan and I can't do this exercise. Can you help _____ ?

4 These are my new trousers. Do you like _____ ?

5 He's a good teacher, but I don't like _____ very much! | 4 |

b Complete the sentences. Use the present simple form of the verbs.

1 Switch if off, Jane! You ___watch___ (watch) too much TV.

2 My uncle _____ (live) in that house over there.

3 Alex and Sarah _____ (play) computer games every weekend.

4 My father _____ (not like) the same music as me.

5 Mike and Alison _____ (not live) with their parents.

6 I _____ (not get up) early at the weekend.

7 Our teacher hardly ever _____ (give) us a lot of homework.

8 _____ you _____ (like) listening to CDs?

9 _____ your mother _____ (work) on Saturdays?

10 _____ they _____ (write) a lot of emails? | 9 |

c Put the words in order to make sentences.

1 never / fish / eat / We
We never eat fish.

2 friend / is / My / late for school / always
_____

3 usually / I / watch / don't / football
_____

4 good / You / usually / at / are / Geography
_____

5 coffee / My / hardly / father / ever / drinks
_____

6 twice / a sports club / I / to / a week / go
_____ | 5 |

d Complete the sentences. Use the present simple or present continuous form of the verbs.

1 Annie often ___plays___ (play) football, but now she *'s playing* (play) computer games.

2 My mum usually _____ (work) in London, but this week she _____ (work) in New York.

3 I _____ (read) a magazine at the moment. It's strange, because I _____ usually _____ (not read) magazines.

4 My grandmother _____ (cook) chicken today. She _____ (cook) lunch for us every Sunday.

5 We _____ (not watch) television very often, but we _____ (watch) an interesting programme at the moment.

6 A: _____ your friends always _____ (swim) in the sea?
   B: No, not always. They _____ (swim) in the pool today. | 10 |

e (Circle) the correct words.

1 She's buying *a / (some)* fruit at the supermarket.

2 Can I have *a / an* orange, please?

3 I can't buy it. I haven't got *much / many* money.

4 How *much / many* tomatoes have we got?

5 *Much / Many* people live in this city.

6 If you want something to eat, have *a / some* sandwich.

7 We've got *a / some* eggs, but we haven't got *much / many* bread. | 7 |

2 **Vocabulary**

a Put the letters in order to find nine more school subjects.

1 trA   *Art*

2 marDa   _____

3 sthMa   _____

4 shinglE   _____

5 niecSec   _____

6 ortHiys   _____

7 rnecFh   _____

8 agGyehorp   _____

9 mInnorafoti noyTecoghl _____

10 Plyasich dEnucioat _____ | 9 |

b) Write the words/phrases in the lists.
Then add three more to each list.

> doing the ironing   ~~listening to music~~   dancing
> cleaning the windows   tidying up   playing the guitar

Hobbies and interests

listening to music

....

....

....

....

Housework

....

....

....

....

....

| 11 |

c) Fill in the puzzle with words for food and drink.
What's the mystery word?

1 | s | u | g | a | r |

2

3

4

5

6

7

8

9

10

1 A lot of people put this in coffee.
2 Chicken and beef, for example.
3 These vegetables sometimes make you cry!
4 You need .... to make toast.
5 I'd like a glass of mineral ....
6 Would you like some fruit .... to drink?
7 This orange vegetable grows under the ground.
8 Fish and .... is a popular take-away meal in Britain.
9 This fruit has got about 80 calories – an ....
10 Would you like vegetables or .... with your meal?

| 9 |

3 Everyday English

Complete the dialogue with the words in the box.

> So what   What about
> check out   ~~guy~~   Let's
> an angel   must be crazy

Bill: Hannah, look! Can you see that [1] _guy_ over there?

Hannah: Yes, I can see him. [2] .... him?

Bill: I think he's looking at you.

Hannah: Really? I don't think so.

Bill: Yes, he is. [3] .... go and talk to him.

Hannah: Bill! You [4] .... ! I don't want to talk to him! He's about 20 years old!

Bill: [5] .... ? Perhaps he's a really nice guy.

Hannah: No, thanks. Bill, can we go? I want to [6] .... the new café.

Bill: Good idea. I'll buy you an ice cream, OK?

Hannah: Thanks, Bill. You're [7] .... !

| 6 |

How did you do?

Tick (✓) a box for each section.

Total score	😊	😐	🙁
70	Very good	OK	Not very good
Grammar	26 – 35	19 – 25	less than 19
Vocabulary	21 – 29	16 – 20	less than 16
Everyday English	4 – 6	3	less than 3

Module 2
Follow your dreams

YOU WILL LEARN ABOUT ...

- A woman who lived in a tree ....
- A special friendship ....
- How British teenagers use mobile phones ....
- The secrets of success ....
- A family who went back in time ....
- Songwriting for a band ....
- Pop idols in Britain ....

  ✱ Can you match each photo with a topic?

YOU WILL LEARN HOW TO ...

Speak
- Talk about when and where you were born
- Give a presentation about your hero
- Describe events in the past
- Discuss sports
- Re-tell a story in the past
- Talk about things you have to do at home
- Talk about a job you'd like to do
- Talk about sleep and dreams

Write
- A poster about your hero
- An email about a day or weekend you enjoyed
- A description of someone's job
- A story

Read
- An article about a woman who saved a tree
- A story about friendship
- An article about using mobile phones
- An article about 'The 1900 House'
- A magazine interview about songwriting
- An article about dreaming up new ideas
- An article about a TV pop music show

Listen
- A presentation about someone's hero
- A dialogue about a TV comedy story
- A presentation about success
- An interview about writing a song
- A song
- Instructions for creating a scene

Use grammar

Can you match the names of the grammar points with the examples?

Past simple: *be*   Is this book **yours**?
Past simple: regular verbs   We haven't got **any** butter.
Past simple: irregular verbs   Julia **lived** in a tree-house.
have to / don't have to   The helicopter **was** very noisy.
some and *any*   Tom **doesn't have to** wear a uniform.
Possessive pronouns   They **met** in the 1936 Olympic Games.

Use vocabulary

Can you think of two more examples for each topic?

Phrasal verbs	Sports	Jobs	Sleeping and waking
climb up	basketball	pilot	go to bed
come down	squash	nurse	go to sleep
....	....	....	....
....	....	....	....

(5) My hero!

* Past simple: *be* and regular verbs,
  was born / were born
* Vocabulary: phrasal verbs (1)

1 Read and listen

(a) Look at the photos and the title of the text.
Why do you think the woman is in the tree?
Read the text quickly to check your ideas.

THE WOMAN WHO LIVED IN A TREE

Julia Hill, an American woman, was born in 1974. She was
23 years old when she discovered that a company wanted
to cut down part of a forest in California. In the forest there
were lots of redwood trees. One of the trees was 70 metres
tall and 1,000 years old.

Julia wasn't happy about this. She travelled to California
and climbed up the tree. 'If I sit in the tree,' she said, 'the
company can't cut it down.' At the beginning, Julia planned
to stay in the tree for two weeks. She lived in a small tree-
house and her friends were very helpful – they cooked food for
her every day. She used her mobile phone to talk to her
family and to news reporters. She stayed in the tree day
and night.

Environmental organisations supported her,
but other people weren't on her side and they
tried to stop her. The company used a
helicopter that stayed near her tree-house for
a long time. The helicopter was very noisy and
there was a lot of wind. Julia didn't like it, but
she stayed in the tree.

In the end, she was successful. The
company agreed not to cut down the redwood.
Finally, after two years and eight days in the tree,
Julia Hill climbed down and walked on the ground
again. She and her friends were very happy.

(b) 🔊 Now read the text again and listen. How do you
say the underlined words in your language?

1   ... a company wanted to cut down part of a forest
    (paragraph 1)
2   Environmental organisations (paragraph 3)
3   The helicopter was very noisy and there was a lot of
    wind. (paragraph 3)
4   The company agreed not to cut down the redwood.
    (paragraph 4)

(c) Answer the questions.

1   What do you know about the tree?
2   How long was Julia up the tree?
3   Who cooked her food for her?
4   How did she talk to people when
    she was in the tree?
5   Who tried to stop her? How?

(d) What do you think Julia did after she
climbed down from the tree?

2 Grammar

Past simple: the verb *be*

(a) Look at the text on page 50. <u>Underline</u> examples of the past simple of the verb *be*.

(b) Complete the table.

Positive	Negative	Question	Short answer
I/he/she/it **was**	I/he/she/it _____ (was not)	_____ I/he/she/it?	Yes, I/he/she/it _____ . No, I/he/she/it _____ (was not).
you/we/they **were**	you/we/they _____ (were not)	_____ you/we/they?	Yes, you/we/they _____ . No, you/we/they _____ (were not).

(c) Complete the sentences with *was, wasn't, were* or *weren't*.

1 Julia Hill ___*was*___ an American woman.
2 There _____ lots of trees in the forest.
3 One tree _____ a thousand years old.
4 Julia _____ happy about the company's plans.
5 Some people helped her, but other people _____ on her side.

(d) Complete the questions with *Was* or *Were*.

1 ___*Was*___ Julia Hill British?
2 _____ the redwood tree very old?
3 _____ Julia's friends helpful?
4 _____ the helicopter very noisy?
5 _____ Julia and her supporters unhappy in the end?

(e) Work with a partner. Ask and answer the questions in Exercise 2d.

A: *Was Julia Hill British?*
B: *No, she wasn't. She was American.*

4 Grammar

was born / were born

Look at the example. Complete the sentences with your information.

Julia Hill was born in 1974. She was born in the USA.

1 I was born in _____ (year).
2 I was born in _____ (place).

5 Speak

(a) Ask other students.

When were you born?
Where were you born?

(b) Work with a partner. Ask and answer about family members.

A: *When was your sister born?*
B: *In 1998. Where were your parents born?*
A: *My mother was born in Rome and my father ...*

3 Pronunciation

was and *were*

(a) 🔊 Listen to the sentences. What vowel sound do you hear? Listen again and repeat.

1 Julia <u>was</u> an American woman.
2 There <u>were</u> lots of trees in the forest.
3 <u>Was</u> the helicopter very noisy?
4 <u>Were</u> the trees very old?

(b) 🔊 Listen and tick (✓) the vowel sound you hear. Then listen again and repeat.

	/ɒ/	/ɜː/	/ə/
1 I <u>was</u> unhappy.	☐	☐	✓
2 He <u>wasn't</u> a good teacher.	☐	☐	☐
3 My friends <u>weren't</u> at the park.	☐	☐	☐
4 We <u>were</u> late yesterday.	☐	☐	☐
5 <u>Was</u> it noisy?	☐	☐	☐
6 Yes, it <u>was</u>.	☐	☐	☐
7 <u>Were</u> you on the bus?	☐	☐	☐
8 Yes, we <u>were</u>.	☐	☐	☐

6 Grammar

Past simple: regular verbs

a Look back at the text on page 50. Find the past simple form of these verbs.

climb	_climbed_
cook	....
live	....
plan	....
stay	....
travel	....
try	....
use	....
walk	....
want	....

b Look at the verbs in Exercise 6a. Complete the rule.

> **Rule:** We use the past simple to talk about finished actions in the past.
>
> With regular verbs, we usually add .... to the verb (*walk – walked, cook – cooked*).
>
> If the verb ends in *e* (for example, *live*), we add ....
>
> If a short verb ends in vowel + consonant (for example, *plan*), we double the .... and add *ed*.
>
> If the verb ends in consonant + *y* (for example, *try*), we change the *y* to .... and add ....

c Complete the sentences. Use the past simple form of the verbs.

1 I .... (want) to go to the cinema last night.
2 When I was young, my family .... (live) in London.
3 Last week we .... (plan) our summer holiday.
4 I .... (try) to phone you yesterday, but nobody .... (answer).
5 Last year we .... (travel) to the USA and we .... (visit) the White House.
6 When I .... (play) with the baby, he .... (stop) crying and .... (smile) at me.

d Look at the example and complete the table.

*Julia **didn't like** it, but she stayed in the tree.*

Positive	Negative
I/he/she/it/you/we/they want**ed**	I/he/she/it/you/we/they .... want

e Complete the sentences. Use the past simple form of the verbs in the box.

> stop   start   talk   tidy   stay   rain   study
> not clean   not finish   not like   not watch   not play   not say

1 I ___started___ a painting but I _didn't finish_ it.
2 They .... in an expensive hotel, but they .... the food.
3 It .... all day on Saturday, so we .... tennis.
4 Helena .... TV last night. She .... for her test.
5 I .... my room, but I .... the windows.
6 He .... for a long time, but he .... anything interesting! We .... listening to him.

7 Pronunciation

-ed endings

🔊 Listen to the words and write them in the lists.

> walked   visited   listened   wanted   watched
> climbed   started   tried   hated   decided

/d/ or /t/	/ɪd/
walked	_visited_
....	....
....	....
....	....
....	....

8 Vocabulary

Phrasal verbs (1)

a Look at the examples from the text on page 50.

*Julia **climbed up** the tree.*
*They wanted to **cut down** part of a forest.*

Can you think of any other verbs that we can use with *up* and *down*?

b 🔊 Match the sentences with the pictures. Then listen, check and repeat.

1 Climb up!
2 Pick it up, please.
3 Put them on.
4 Get in.
5 Polly! Come down!
6 Put that knife down.
7 Take it off!
8 Get out!

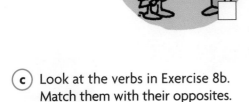

c Look at the verbs in Exercise 8b. Match them with their opposites.

climb up – come down

d Work with a partner. Think of different situations where you can use the phrasal verbs in Exercise 8b.

9 Listen

a Amy made a poster about her hero for a class presentation. Look at the poster and the sentences. How many of the sentences can you complete?

b 🔊 Listen to Amy's presentation. Find information to complete the other sentences in Exercise 9a.

c Why is Chico Mendes Amy's hero?

MY HERO: CHICO MENDES

born: 1944 in Brazil

worked as a rubber farmer in the Amazon

wanted to stop people from cutting down the trees

died in 1988

1 Chico Mendes was born in _____ , in _____ .
2 _____ helped him to learn to read and write.
3 He visited the USA in 19_____ .
4 He visited the USA because _____ .
5 He died in 19_____ .
6 _____ killed him.
7 After Chico Mendes died, _____ .

Who's your hero?

10 Read and listen

a 🔊 Look at the photo story. Who is Lucy's hero, and why? Read, listen and check your answers.

1

Lucy: That was a great presentation, Amy.

Amy: Thanks. I enjoyed doing it.

2

Amy: So who's your hero, Lucy?

Lucy: My grandfather.

Amy: Your grandfather? You can't be serious!

3

Lucy: Why not? My grandfather was a firefighter in London. He saved loads of people and he's got a lot of medals.

4

Amy: Is that right?

Lucy: Yes, he was a firefighter for 40 years, and after he stopped working, he was a volunteer in children's hospitals.

5

Amy: That's amazing. I'd really like to meet him.

Lucy: OK. We can go to his house together one day.

Amy: Great!

b Mark the statements
T (true) or *F* (false).

1 Lucy's grandfather is
a firefighter. ☐

2 He worked as a
volunteer in
children's hospitals. ☐

3 Lucy would like to
take Amy to his
house in the future. ☐

4 Amy doesn't want
to visit him. ☐

c Why do you think
Amy says 'You can't
be serious!' in photo 2?

11 Everyday English

a Find the expressions in the photo story. Who says them?
How do you say them in your language?

1 You can't be serious   3 That's amazing
2 loads of people   4 one day

b Read the dialogues. Fill in the spaces with the underlined
expressions from Exercise 11a.

1 **Anne:** I'd really like to travel in the future.
Gina: Yes, me too. I'd love to go to India ....

2 **Hugo:** Why can't you come to the cinema tonight?
Adam: Because I've got .... homework to do.

3 **René:** I'm going to a party on Thursday night at Carlo's house.
Marta: .... ! We've got two tests at school on Friday.

4 **Martina:** He only started learning English one year ago and his
English is excellent!
Simon: Only one year? ....

12 Write

a Read the text that Dave wrote about his hero. Match the questions
with the paragraphs. Write the numbers 1–3 in the boxes.

a What did this person do? ☐
b Why is this person a hero for you? ☐
c Who is your hero? ☐

1 My hero is Helen Thayer. She was the first woman who
walked to the North Pole alone.

2 Helen Thayer was born in New Zealand and she lived
there when she was a girl. Later, she lived in Guatemala
for four years and then in the United States. When she
was fifty, she had a dream. She wanted to walk to the
North Pole alone, and she decided to do it. On her
journey, Helen didn't have any help. She was completely
alone except for her dog, Charlie, a Canadian husky.
The journey was very difficult. She walked 345 miles
in temperatures of −50°! Once, seven polar bears
attacked Helen and Charlie. Charlie saved Helen's life.

3 Helen Thayer is my hero because she had a dream
and she was determined to make it come true.
She was always positive, even in very dangerous and
difficult situations.

b Write three paragraphs about your hero. Use Dave's example
to help you.

c Make a poster about your hero. Then give a presentation
to the class.

For your portfolio

(6) Good friends

* Past simple: regular and irregular verbs
* Vocabulary: past time expressions, sports

Read and listen

(a) How many Olympic sports do you know? What are your favourite Olympic sports?

(b) Read about two athletes in the 1936 Olympic Games. What was the sport and who was the winner?

(c) ◁)) Now read the text again and listen. Put the pictures in the order that you hear them. Write the numbers 1–4 in the boxes.

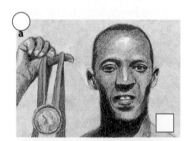
a

b

c

d

The start of a great friendship

Jesse Owens

In the 1936 Olympic Games in Berlin, there were only two athletes with a chance to win the gold medal in the final of the long jump. One was Lutz Long, a German long jumper, and the other was Jesse Owens, a black American from Cleveland. Adolf Hitler, the leader of Nazi Germany, was in the stadium and he wanted Lutz Long to win.

At the beginning of the competition, Jesse Owens had some problems because he stepped over the white line twice. Everybody in the stadium thought that Lutz Long was going to win. But then something surprising happened. Lutz Long went to talk to Owens to help him. Owens listened to what Long told him. In his next jump, Owens didn't step over the line and his jump was good. The next two jumps by both athletes were excellent and everybody in the stadium was very excited. But finally, with his last jump, Owens beat Long by 27 centimetres and won the gold medal. This was the second of the four gold medals that Jesse Owens won in the 1936 Olympics.

Adolf Hitler was very angry and he left the stadium. The first person to shake hands with Owens was Lutz Long. The two men became good friends, and they stayed friends after the Olympics.

A short time before he died in 1979, Jesse Owens talked about what happened in the Berlin Olympics. He said, 'I won four gold medals in Berlin, but I won something much better and more important than that: Lutz Long's friendship.'

Lutz Long

(d) What do you think Long said to Owens after Owens stepped over the line? Why do you think Long helped Owens?

2 Grammar

Past simple: regular and irregular verbs

a Look at the examples. How are the verbs in 1 different from the verbs in 2?

1 He **stepped** over the white line twice.
   They **stayed** friends for the rest of their lives.
   He **died** in 1979.

2 Jesse Owens **had** some problems.
   Lutz Long **went** to talk to Owens.
   Owens **beat** Long.

b Put the verbs in the past simple and write them in the lists. Use the text on page 56 to help you.

~~stay~~	~~have~~	tell	leave	say	step
become	beat	want	win	listen
think	happen	go	talk	die

Regular verbs	Irregular verbs
stayed	_had_

c Complete the summary.
Use the verbs in the past simple.

Jesse Owens and Lutz Long ¹ _were_ (be) in the long jump final of the 1936 Olympic Games in Berlin. Jesse Owens ² _____ (have) some problems at the start of the competition and everybody in the stadium ³ _____ (think) that Lutz Long was going to win. Then Long ⁴ _____ (go) to talk to Owens. Their next two jumps ⁵ _____ (be) both good. It ⁶ _____ (be) a very exciting competition. Owen ⁷ _____ (win) the gold medal with his last jump. After this, Long and Owens ⁸ _____ (become) very good friends. Owens ⁹ _____ (die) in 1979.

Past simple: questions

d Look at the examples and complete the table.

Did Long **beat** Owens?   No, he **didn't**.
Did Owens **go** to Berlin in 1936?   Yes, he **did**.

Question	Short answer
_____ I/you/ we/they/he/she/it go?	Yes, I/you/we/they/he/she/it _____ . No, I/you/we/they/he/she/it _____ (did not).

e Put the words in the correct order to make questions.

1 you / out / go / last night / did ?

   ....

2 music / you / last weekend / did / listen to ?

   ....

3 coffee / you / this morning / drink / did ?

   ....

4 you / watch / yesterday / did / TV ?

   ....

5 on holiday / you / last year / did / go ?

   ....

3 Speak

a Work with a partner. Ask and answer the questions from Exercise 2e.

A: Did you go out last night?
B: No, I didn't. I stayed at home and watched TV.

b Work with a new partner. Tell him/her about your first partner's answers.

Antonia didn't go out last night. She stayed at home and watched TV.

4 Vocabulary

Past time expressions

(a) *When we talk about the past, we can use time expressions like these:*

yesterday
yesterday morning/afternoon/evening

last night   last week/month/year
last Saturday   last April

an hour ago   four days ago
ten years ago

How do you say these things in your language?

(b) Complete the sentences with your own information.

1 Four hours ago, I was ....
....

2 Last night I went to bed at ....
....

3 Yesterday evening I ....
....

4 Last Saturday I ....
....

5 Eight years ago I was ....
....

6 My last holiday was ....
....

(c) Complete the sentences.
Use a time expression with *ago*.

1 David is fifteen now. He started school when he was five.
David started school
ten years ago.................................... .

2 I met your cousin last Saturday. It's Wednesday today.
I met your cousin ....
....

3 It's 10.30 now. My English class began at 9.30.
My English class began ....
....

4 The school holidays started at the end of June. It's the end of August now.
The school holidays started
....

5 I ate my lunch at one o'clock today. It's six o'clock now.
I ate my lunch
....

5 Speak

Work with a partner. Ask and answer the past simple questions. Use *ago* in your answers.

When / start school?
When / begin learning English?
When / arrive at school this morning?
When / meet your best friend?

A: *When did you start school?*
B: *Nine years ago. When did you ...?*

6 Vocabulary

Sports

(a) 🔊 Write the words under the pictures. Then listen, check and repeat.

basketball   cycling   ice hockey   skiing   skateboarding
snowboarding   surfing   ~~swimming~~   volleyball

① *swimming*   ②   ③

④   ⑤   ⑥

⑦   ⑧   ⑨

(b) Work with a partner or in a group.
Answer the questions about the sports in Exercise 6a.

Which sports ...

1 always have teams?
2 have equipment with wheels?
3 are water sports?
4 are in the Winter Olympics?
5 are popular in your country?
6 do you do?
7 do you like watching?

7 Listen

(a) Look at the pictures of four people in a TV programme and read their names.

 Jane

 Louise

Danny

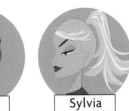 Sylvia

(b) Work with a partner. Put the pictures in order to make a story. Write 1–8 in the boxes.

a   BOX OFFICE NOW OPEN

b

c   7

d

e

f

g

h

(c) Before you listen, check that you know what these words mean.

> go out with someone   push   pour
> have an argument   cream cake

(d) 🔊 Listen to the dialogue about the TV programme. Check your answers to Exercise 7b.

8 Speak

(a) Work with a partner. Re-tell the story. Use the pictures to help you.

(b) Were Jane and Louise right to do this to Danny? Discuss this with your partner.

9 Pronunciation Word stress

(a) 🔊 Look at the list. How many syllables has each word got? Listen and check.

1 surfing ....   4 cycling ....
2 basketball ....   5 skateboarding ....
3 sport ....   6 Olympics ....

(b) 🔊 Write the words in the lists. Then listen again and check.

●   ●●   ●●●   ●●●

....

....

10 Read

(a) Look at the pictures. Can you understand the message on the mobile phone? Read the text quickly and check your ideas.

Using mobile phones

Text messaging

Clare is 15 and she lives in Leeds, in the north of England. It's Saturday and Clare is shopping. She wants to get in touch with her friend, Jamie, so she takes out her mobile phone. But she doesn't phone him – she sends him a text message. This is what Clare wants to say:

Hi Jamie
Are you OK? I'm great. Please call me before tomorrow. Thanks. See you!

But this is what she sends:

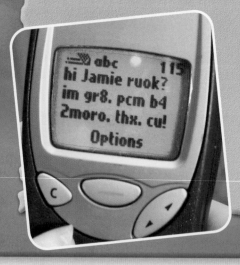

To keep in touch with their friends, British teenagers often use text messaging because it's quick, easy and cheap – and there is now a special kind of written language that they use. The important thing is to make messages short. Here are some examples of how text messages make language shorter.

ruok?	=	Are you OK?
pls	=	please
2day	=	today
2nite	=	tonight
2moro	=	tomorrow
b4	=	before
l8	=	late
gr8	=	great
thx	=	thanks
pcm	=	Please call me
ilu	=	I love you
cu	=	See you
hand	=	Have a nice day
b4n	=	Bye for now

Of course, this kind of writing is only for text messaging. Clare and her friends don't write like this when they are doing school work or writing letters.

Mobiles at school

In Britain, where 50% of the population now own mobile phones, about eight million users are of school age. This number is growing, not only among teenagers, but among children under 13.

At school there can be problems with ringing phones and students sending text messages in class. Most schools have a rule that students must turn off their mobiles in class time – they can only use them at break, at lunch time or after school. If a student's phone rings during class, the teacher can take it away. Other schools ban mobiles completely.

(b) Now read the text again. Answer the questions.

1 Where is Clare when she sends a message to Jamie?
2 Why do teenagers use text messaging to 'talk' to friends?
3 What problems are there with mobile phones in class?
4 When can most students use their mobile phones at school?

(c) What does this text message say? Use the text to help you.

> hi Matt
> how ru? im in town 2day. ru going 2 Steve's party 2moro? do u wan2 buy a present 4 him? pcm b4 2nite. b4n. hand! Mike

11 Write

Do one of these two activities.

(a) Look again at pictures a–h on page 59. Imagine you're one of the people in the story. Write a diary entry about what happened.

(b) Read the email from Alison to her penfriend, Julia. Answer the questions.

1 Where did Alison go at the weekend?
2 What did she do there?
3 What does she ask Julia to send her?

Previous ▼   Next ▼   Reply   Reply All   Print

Hi Julia!

How are you? Did you have a good holiday in California? Can you send me some of your photos in your next email?

I had a really good weekend. My brother and I went to my cousin's house in London. We went on the train on Friday evening and arrived at six o'clock. My aunt and uncle cooked a big dinner for us, and then we all went bowling. It was my first time, so I wasn't very good and I didn't win, but it was good fun. On Saturday we went shopping in Oxford Street. I bought some new summer clothes and my brother bought a computer game (a football game, of course!). In the evening we all went to a nice Italian restaurant. I had a pizza and it was delicious. We went home on Sunday but I wanted to stay in London – I like it there.

My mum is calling me, so I can't write any more. Write soon and tell me all about your holiday, and don't forget the photos!

Love,

Alison

Write a similar email to a penfriend. Tell him/her about a weekend or day you enjoyed. Use Alison's email to help you.

They say this stops students wasting time in class. They also say it helps to stop people who want to steal mobiles and wait for students on their way home.

Most students think they should be able to bring their phones to school. Clare says 'There's no reason to ban mobiles at school. They're very useful. And I feel safe if I've got a phone in my pocket or in my bag. If there's any trouble, I can always get in touch with my parents.'

(d) Do you agree with Clare's opinion in the last paragraph of the text?

For your portfolio

7 The secrets of success

* have to / don't have to
* Vocabulary: jobs

1 Read and listen

(a) Look at the photos. Match the people with the jobs. Write 1–6 in the boxes.

| 1 model | 2 business person | 3 film star |
| 4 singer | 5 sports person | 6 writer |

Read the text quickly.

Bill Gates

David Beckham

Penelope Cruz

J. K. Rowling

Naomi Campbell

Robbie Williams

Why are they so successful?

These people are different in a lot of ways. Some of them are men and some are women. They come from different countries, they have different interests and they have different professions.

But there's one thing that they have in common – they are all extremely successful and they are at the top of their professions.

An interesting question is: *why* are they so successful? A lot of people think that the answer is talent – a special ability to do something very well. But perhaps this is not the answer. Some of these people are not unusually talented. They're good at what they do, of course, but they aren't always excellent. Also, there are lots of people who have talent but who don't become very successful.

So if the answer to the question isn't talent, what *is* the answer?

(b) 🔊 Now read the text again and listen. Answer the questions.

1 In what ways are the six people different?
2 All six people also have something in common. What is it?
3 Look at the question in the title. What do a lot of people think the answer is?

(c) What do you think people need to be successful? Tick the things that you think are necessary. Then compare ideas with a partner.

being lucky	☐	having a dream	☐
being determined	☐	having rich parents	☐
having lots of money	☐	getting good school results	☐
being hard-working	☐	having good friends	☐

(d) 🔊 Alex did a school project on 'Successful people'. Listen to the last part of his presentation. What does he think successful people need? Are his ideas the same as yours?

(e) Think of someone you know who is successful but not famous. In what ways is this person successful? Discuss your ideas with a partner.

2 Grammar

have to / don't have to

a Look at the examples. Complete the rule and the table.

You **have to** be determined.   You **don't have to** get good school results.
You **have to** have a dream.   You **don't have to** work 24 hours a day.

Rule: We use _____ to say 'This is necessary'.
We use _____ to say 'This isn't necessary'.

Positive	Negative	Question	Short answer
I/you/we/they **have to** go	I/you/we/they _____ (do not) have to go	_____ I/you/we/they **have to** go?	Yes, I/you/we/they _____ . No, I/you/we/they _____ (do not).
he/she/it _____ go	he/she/it _____ (does not) have to go	_____ he/she/it **have to** go?	Yes, he/she/it _____ . No, he/she/it _____ (does not).

b Complete the sentences. Use *have/has to* or *don't/doesn't have to*.

1 If you want to work in the USA, you _____ speak good English.

2 My sister has got a young baby, so she often _____ get up during the night.

3 My friend gets good test results, but he _____ work very hard. In fact, he never studies before a test.

4 Tomorrow is Sunday, so I _____ go to school. Great!

5 At our school we _____ wear a uniform. It's dark blue with a white shirt.

6 At my cousins' school they _____ wear a uniform. They can wear what they want.

3 Pronunciation

have to

 Usually, *have* has a /v/ sound, but in *have to / don't have to*, it has a /f/ sound. Also *to* has the weak sound /ə/.

Listen and repeat the sentences.

1 I have to go.
2 You don't have to shout.
3 He doesn't have to come.
4 We have to learn English.
5 You have to have money.
6 Does she have to work hard?

4 Speak

a Write ✓ for the things you have to do at home. Write ✗ for the things you don't have to do.

☐ do the washing-up

☐ tidy my bedroom

☐ get up early on weekdays

☐ do the cooking

☐ clean the bathroom

☐ do the ironing

b Work with a partner. Ask and answer questions about the activities in Exercise 4a.

A: *Do you have to do the washing-up?*
B: *Yes, I do. What about you?*
A: *Sometimes, but I don't have to do the cooking.*

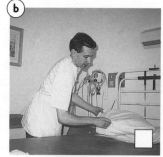

a · b · c · d

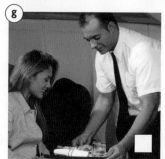

e · f · g · h

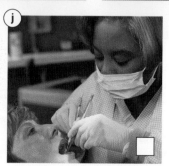

i · j

5 Vocabulary

Jobs

a 🔊 Match the names of the jobs with the pictures. Write 1–10 in the boxes. Then listen, check and repeat.

> 1 engineer   2 teacher
> 3 nurse   4 vet   5 doctor
> 6 flight attendant
> 7 lawyer   8 pilot
> 9 dentist   10 secretary

b Write the names of four more jobs you are interested in. Use a dictionary or ask your teacher.

1 ....
2 ....
3 ....
4 ....

c 🔊 Listen to four teenagers. Which job does each one want to do in the future?
Fill in the spaces with four of the jobs in the box.

> singer   doctor   lawyer
> teacher   pilot   tennis player
> vet   computer programmer

1 Mike: ....
2 Tina: ....
3 Tony: ....
4 Judith: ....

6 Speak

a 🔊 Read the dialogue between two students. Fill in the spaces with the phrases from the box. Then listen and check your answers.

> speak English   be a pilot   not sure   get good school results
> leave school   I'd like   Maths and Physics   have to do

Jenny: What do you want to be when you ¹.............................. ?

Mark: I want to ².............................. .

Jenny: Really? What do you ³.............................. for that?

Mark: Well, you have to ⁴.............................. and you have to be good at ⁵.............................. . And you have to ⁶..............................
really well too. What about you? What do you want to do?

Jenny: I'm ⁷.............................. , but I think ⁸..............................
to be a vet.

b Work with a partner. Continue the dialogue between Jenny and Mark. Use the phrases in the box. Then practise the whole dialogue.

> like animals   study for five years   get good results
> be good at Medicine

c Work with a different partner. Find out about what he/she wants to be. Use the dialogue between Jenny and Mark to help you.

7 Read

a This text is about a family who lived like people in 1900. What do you think it says about:

- the house they lived in?
- housework?
- clothes?

Read the text quickly and check your ideas.

The 1900 House

In 1999, a television company in Britain made a very popular programme called *The 1900 House*. They changed an ordinary house in a street in London so it was the same as a house from the year 1900. For example, it had no electricity, just gas for the lights and the kitchen. The toilet was outside in the garden, and all the furniture was from 1900 or before.

Then they found a family – the Bowlers – to live in the house for three months. Six people in the family lived in the house: Paul and Joyce Bowler, their daughters, Kathryn, Ruth and Hilary and their son, Joe. For three months, while they were living in the house, they had to wear Victorian clothes and live like people at that time. For example, they had to wash their hair with egg and lemon, not shampoo. They had to wash their clothes by hand because they didn't have a washing machine, and they had to use the toilet outside in the garden. But the family didn't have to go shopping because the TV company did all their shopping for them.

There were cameras inside the house to film the family's everyday life, and the Bowlers talked on television about their experiences. Here are some of the things that Hilary said later about her time in the house:

'Some things were difficult – we had to find things to do in the evenings, because there was no television or computer, and we all had to work hard to clean the house and to cook our food. My sister and I had to share a bedroom and a bed, too! It was fun – and we didn't have to go to school every day, that was nice. But I don't want to do it again. I think I'd like to live in the future, not the past!'

b Now read the text again and answer the questions.

1. How many people lived in the house?
2. How long did they live there for?
3. Why was there a camera inside the house?

c Make a list of things that the Bowlers had to do and didn't have to do. Use the words in the box.

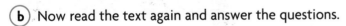

~~egg and lemon~~ toilet bed school clothes shopping

*They **had to** wash their hair with egg and lemon.*

d Look at your list from Exercise 7c. Write sentences about the things you have to do and don't have to do.

I don't have to wash my hair with egg and lemon.

Look

Present
I **have to** do a lot of housework.
I **don't have to** do the cooking.

Past
We all **had to** work hard.
The family **didn't have to** go shopping.

e Hilary said: 'I think I'd like to live in the future, not the past!' Do you agree with her? Would you like to go back in time like the Bowlers? Why / Why not?

It's my dream

8 Read and listen

a 🔊 Look at the photo story. What's Amy's dream? Read and listen to find the answer.

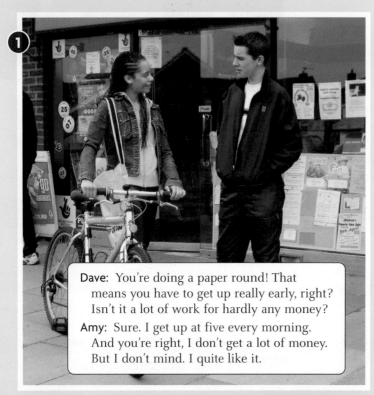

1

Dave: You're doing a paper round! That means you have to get up really early, right? Isn't it a lot of work for hardly any money?

Amy: Sure. I get up at five every morning. And you're right, I don't get a lot of money. But I don't mind. I quite like it.

2

Dave: Like it? But you have to cycle round the town in the cold and in the rain.

Amy: That's right. But I'm doing it for a reason!

Dave: Yeah? What's that?

3

Amy: Well, I'm saving up for a good guitar. I don't get a lot of pocket money, so I have to work. I want to be a singer. It's my dream.

Dave: Your dream?

4 ?

Amy: Yes. Singing in a band. That's my dream. What's yours?

Dave: Um ... well ... that's a good question. I'm not really sure ...

b Answer the questions.

1 What job does Amy do?
2 What does Dave think about Amy's job?
3 Does Amy work when the weather is bad?
4 What does Amy want to buy?
5 Has Dave got a dream?

c Discuss these questions.

1 Do teenagers sometimes work in your country?
2 If they do, what kind of jobs do they get?
3 Do you have a job?
4 What do you think are good jobs for teenagers? What are bad jobs? Why?

9 Everyday English

a Find expressions 1–4 in the photo story and match them with expressions a–d.

1	doing a paper round	a	money your parents give you
2	hardly any money	b	almost no money
3	saving up	c	taking newspapers to people's houses
4	pocket money	d	putting money in the bank because you want to buy something

b Read the dialogues. Fill in the spaces with expressions 1–4 from Exercise 9a.

1 **Diane:** Why are you _____ ? You have to get up really early!
   Peter: I really want to buy a new stereo, so I'm _____ . I've got nearly €100 now.

2 **Carol:** Tom buys new clothes every week!
   Franco: That's because he gets a lot of _____ from his parents.

3 **Joanne:** Those shoes look perfect with your dress.
   Paula: But I've got _____ . I can't buy them.

10 Write

a Read the questions Hakan asked his uncle. Then read what he wrote about his uncle's job. Match the questions with the paragraphs. Write 1–3 in the boxes.

a What do you like and dislike about your job? ☐

b Why did you decide to be a dentist, and what did you have to do to get the job? ☐

c What do you have to do in your job? ☐

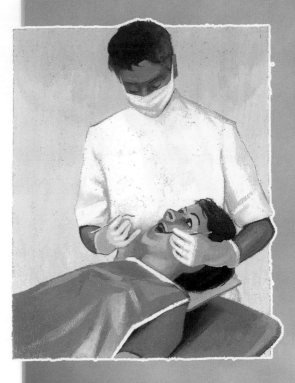

1 When he was young, my uncle Erol always wanted to be a policeman, but when he was 18, he decided to be a dentist because dentists get more money. To be a dentist, he had to study hard for five years at university and take a lot of exams.

2 In his job my uncle has to clean and fix people's teeth, and sometimes he has to pull them out! He doesn't have to get up very early but he has to work hard, usually from 10.00 in the morning to 7.30 in the evening from Monday to Saturday.

3 He likes his job because he never has to take his work home, and he meets lots of people. One thing he doesn't like is that he can't really talk to his patients, because he is working inside their mouths!

b Ask a friend or family member about his/her job. Then write about the information you get. Use Hakan's questions and text to help you.

For your portfolio

8 New ideas

* *some* and *any*, possessive pronouns
* Vocabulary: sleeping and waking

1 Read and listen

(a) Who are your favourite singers? Do they write their own songs? What's your favourite song and why?

(b) Nick plays in the band 4Tune. *COOL* is the name of the magazine at Nick's school. Read the beginning of an interview in the magazine and answer the questions.

1 Who is the main songwriter for 4Tune?
2 Who else writes songs for the band?

(c) 🔊 Now read the text again and listen. Mark the sentences *T* (true) or *F* (false).

1 All the new songs are finished. ☐
2 The interviewer from *COOL* wants to hear the new songs. ☐
3 There's a party at school this month. ☐
4 Karen writes dance songs. ☐
5 The other people in the band help with the songwriting. ☐
6 Nick always enjoys writing songs. ☐
7 Nick wrote *What Makes You Think They're Happy?* when he was at his desk. ☐

4Tune
NEW MUSIC

4Tune are back – with some new songs. We talked to Nick from year 11, a songwriter with the band. Nick has lots of things to do, but *COOL* asked him to give us some time. We wanted some information about the band's new music.

COOL: Nick, tell us about your new songs.

Nick: Well, they aren't all finished. There's still some work to do – you know, the little things you want to change at the last minute. But they're nearly ready.

COOL: We can't wait. When can we hear them?

Nick: We're planning to play them at the school party at the end of next month.

COOL: Great! So let's talk about the music. Do the other band members write any songs? Or are they all yours?

Nick: Well, I write a lot of them, but they're not all mine. Karen writes too – some of the fast dance songs are hers. And we always ask the rest of the band to listen to the songs, and they usually have some good ideas for changes. So in the end, we think the songs belong to all of us – they're ours, not just mine or Karen's.

COOL: Do you like writing songs?

Nick: Yeah, I love it. Well, not always! You know, there are good days and bad days. Sometimes a song is easy to write, but I sometimes sit for hours and I don't get any ideas.

COOL: So do you sit at a desk when you're writing?

Nick: No, not always. I often get ideas when I'm outside, when I'm walking around, so I always have a pen and some paper with me.

COOL: Did you write any of the new songs when you were away from your desk?

Nick: Well, yes, actually. One of them is called *What makes you think they're happy?* and I wrote it after I heard a conversation between two people.

2 Grammar

some and *any*

a Look at the examples from the interview on page 68. Complete the rule.

*We wanted **some** information about the band's new music.*
*They usually have **some** good ideas for changes.*
*I sometimes sit for hours and I don't get **any** ideas.*
*Do the other band members write **any** songs?*

> **Rule:** With uncountable and plural nouns, we use
> .... in positive sentences. We use .... in negative
> sentences and questions.

b Complete the sentences with *some* or *any*.

1 I wanted to buy *some* food, but I didn't have
   .... money.

2 A: Have we got .... homework tonight?
   B: Yes, we've got .... grammar exercises to do.

3 Mario bought .... new jeans last week, but he
   didn't buy .... shoes.

4 A: Let's listen to .... music.
   B: OK. Did you bring .... CDs?

5 I'd like to make .... sandwiches. The problem is:
   I've got .... cheese, but I haven't got .... butter.

3 Speak

Work with a partner.
Student A: Look at the picture of Nick's desk on this page.
Student B: Turn to page 136.

Find out what is different in your partner's picture.
Take it in turns to ask and answer.

A: *Is/Are there any ... in your picture?*
B: *Yes, there's / there are some ...*
   No, there isn't/aren't any ...

4 Grammar

Possessive pronouns

a Look at the examples. Then complete the table.

Do the other band members write any
*songs? Or are they all **yours**?*
I write a lot of them, but they're not
*all **mine**.*
Karen writes too – some of the fast dance
*songs are **hers**.*
*The songs belong to all of us – they're **ours**.*

Subject pronoun	I	you	we	they	he	she
Possessive adjective	my	your	our	their	his	her
Possessive pronoun	......	......	......	theirs	his	......

b Replace the underlined words with possessive pronouns.

1 Hey, Caroline! This isn't my
  pen. Is it <u>your pen</u>?   *yours*

2 Please give this book to
  Steve. I think it's <u>his book</u>.   ....

3 I like your trainers, but I
  prefer <u>her trainers</u>.   ....

4 Our school uniform is awful!
  But I like <u>their uniform</u>.   ....

5 A: I haven't got any paper.
  B: Do you want some
     of <u>my paper</u>?   ....

6 A: My computer doesn't work.
  B: Come over to my place.
     You can use <u>our computer</u>.   ....

5 Listen

(a) 🔊 Nick wrote the song *What Makes You Think They're Happy?* after he heard a conversation. Think about questions 1–3 while you read and listen to the song.

1 Where do you think Nick heard the conversation?
2 Who do you think the two people were?
3 Who do you think *they* are in the song title?

(b) 🔊 Listen to the second part of the interview with Nick. Check your answers to Exercise 5a.

6 Pronunciation

Rhyming words

(a) 🔊 Songwriters often use words that rhyme. These words are all in Nick's song. Match the rhyming pairs. Then listen, check your answers and repeat.

1	plane	a	right
2	fun	b	more
3	floor	c	great
4	late	d	Spain
5	night	e	sun

(b) 🔊 Do the same with these words.

1	keys	a	hurt
2	red	b	please
3	thought	c	run
4	shirt	d	short
5	won	e	said
6	talk	f	fork

What Makes You Think They're Happy?

I clean the tables, clean the floor.
I hate this place, don't want no more
Of this life, of this life.
These people here, they take a plane,
Fly off to France, fly off to Spain.
They're happy, they're happy.

[Chorus]
What makes you think they're happy?
Perhaps it's not so great.
They're looking at their watches
And they're scared they will be late.
What makes you think they're happy?

I want some money, want some fun.
I want to go and find some sun
In this life, in this life.
Look at these guys, they're all right.
They dance and sing, all day, all night.
They're happy, they're happy.

[Chorus]

7 Read

a When do you usually think of new ideas? What do you do when you're thinking hard?

b Read the text about how people think of new ideas. Which picture shows Walt Disney when he was working on an idea?

DREAMING UP NEW IDEAS

Inventors, songwriters, writers and painters – all these people need imagination and ideas. People can get ideas at any time, for example when they are walking down a street or listening to a conversation. Some people get ideas in strange ways. Isaac Newton, for example, discovered the law of universal gravity when he saw an apple falling from a tree. Creative people often get ideas when they are asleep, when they are dreaming or even when they are daydreaming.

Walt Disney, the famous American film-maker, often went into a daydream when he was working and thinking of new ideas. One man who worked with Disney remembers:

'I can see Walt now. We're all in a meeting, seven or eight people are around a table, and suddenly Walt gets an idea. He stops talking. He puts his arms on the table and puts his left hand to his face. He opens his mouth a little. He looks and looks at something, a place high up in the room. This continues for a long time, perhaps ten minutes. Nobody says anything. Then Walt "wakes up", he tells us about the idea for a new cartoon and the meeting goes on.'

8 Vocabulary

Sleeping and waking

a 🔊 Look at the expressions about sleep. Match the opposites. Then listen, check and repeat.

1 to go to bed   a   to wake up
2 to go to sleep   b   to be awake
3 to be asleep   c   to get up

b What's the difference between *dreaming* and *daydreaming*?

c Complete the sentences with the expressions in the box. Use the correct form of the verbs. You can check with the list of irregular verbs on page 138.

> wake up   go to sleep   ~~go to bed~~
> be asleep   get up   be awake
> dream   daydream

1 My mother was very tired last night. She *went to bed* at nine o'clock.
2 Sometimes I go to bed at ten. Then I read a book for an hour and I _____ at about eleven.
3 Last night Lucy _____ about winning the lottery.
4 Please don't talk too loudly. The baby _____ .
5 I didn't sleep at all last night. I _____ all night.
6 This morning I _____ at six o'clock, but I'm lazy, so I stayed in bed and I _____ at eight.
7 Nick doesn't listen to the teacher. He _____ about being a famous singer.

9 Speak

Work with a partner. Ask and answer the questions.

1 What time do you usually go to bed and get up at weekends?
2 What do you do when you can't go to sleep?
3 How often do you daydream? What do you daydream about?
4 Can you remember a dream you had? Tell your partner about it.
   I dreamed I was flying over my city ...

Culture in mind

10 Read

(a) Look at the photographs. Do you know who these people are?

(b) Read the text quickly. What have Will Young and Hear'Say got in common?

Hear'Say

pop idols

Some British pop groups – for example the Beatles and the Rolling Stones, Take That and the Spice Girls – are famous all over the world.

Take That and the Spice Girls started in the 1990s, but these days there is a new way to turn people into pop stars: TV talent shows. That's how the band Hear'Say started. *Popstars* was a TV contest to create a new pop group. Out of hundreds of contestants, the judges chose five young people – and Hear'Say was born. *Popstars* was extremely popular with TV audiences, and it was followed by *Pop Idol*.

Pop Idol started in October 2001 as a programme to find a new solo singer. At the beginning, there were more than 10,000 people who came to audition (these people are often called *wannabes*, from the words *want to be*). After some time there were 50 contestants, and then later only ten. In February 2002, there were only two singers left: Gareth Gates and Will Young. Almost 9 million TV viewers in Britain voted on the final night of the programme, and the winner, with 4.6 million votes, was Will Young.

Some people voted for Will Young because he argued with the judges. The four judges criticised the contestants very strongly, including Will, and some people thought they were cruel. But one of the judges said 'Having a difficult time for two minutes on television – so what? If you don't want that, go to another talent show!'

Will is now a big star. His first record after *Pop Idol* was called *Anything is Possible / Evergreen*, and in Britain it sold over a million copies in one week. He's happy that he didn't go on another talent show. Gareth Gates is happy too – he is also a successful singer now. But the question remains: are TV programmes like *Pop Idol* a good way to find new singers or groups?

Will Young

Will Young & Gareth Gates

c Now read the text again. Mark the statements *T* (true), *F* (false) or *N* (no information in the text).

1 The Spice Girls started in 1996.

2 A lot of people watched *Popstars*.

3 There were 50 contestants at the beginning of *Pop Idol*.

4 On *Pop Idol*, the singers have to answer questions.

5 Gareth Gates got 4.5 million votes.

6 Will Young argued with the judges of *Pop Idol*.

7 He was very successful after *Pop Idol*.

d Are there television programmes likes *Popstars* and *Pop Idol* in your country? If so, are they popular? If not, would you like to have programmes like this?

e What's your answer to the question at the end of the text?

11 Write

a 🔊 Close your eyes. Listen and do what the speaker tells you to do.

b Stefano listened to the same recording and wrote about what he 'saw'. Read his story.

> Stefano (15)
>
> I walked slowly along the beach. I saw the blue sea and white sand, and in the sky I saw a big white bird. There weren't any people on the beach, only me. It was really beautiful.
>
> The tree was tall and thin and it had long branches. The box was old and brown, and it had a key. I saw my name on it in gold letters. When I opened it, I was very surprised because there was a new camera inside. I lost my camera last week, so I was very happy.
>
> I took the camera and went back up the beach. When I looked back, I saw the tree and the big white bird. I took a photo.

c Write a paragraph about what you 'saw' while you were listening to the recording.

What did you see on the beach?   What was your present?

What did your tree look like?   What did you do with it?

What did your box look like?

d Work with a partner. Read your partner's story. What differences are there between the two stories?

Module 2 Check your progress

1 Grammar

a) Complete the dialogue with the past simple form of be.

A: You [1] _weren't_ at school yesterday afternoon. Where [2] _____ you?

B: I [3] _____ at home. There [4] _____ a football match on television.

A: [5] _____ it a good match?

B: No, it [6] _____ ! All the players [7] _____ awful!

| 6 |

b) Complete the sentences. Use the correct form of the verbs in the box.

| win | become | stop | be̶ | be |
| jump | see | win | say |

1 In 1950, there ___were___ 199,854 people at the World Cup Final between Brazil and Uruguay in Rio de Janeiro. They _____ a great match.

2 The Swedish athlete Oskar Gomar Swann _____ famous when he _____ a silver medal in shooting at the Olympic Games in Antwerp in 1920. He _____ 72 years old.

3 At the 1984 Olympic Games in Los Angeles, Carl Lewis _____ four gold medals.

4 In the first round of the long jump, Lewis _____ 8.54 metres. After that, he _____ . 'Nobody can beat me,' he _____ .

| 8 |

c) Complete the sentences with the correct form of the verbs.

1 I ___went___ (go) to the cinema last night, but I _____ (not enjoy) the film very much.

2 What _____ James _____ (say) to you yesterday?

3 A: _____ you _____ (see) Alice last night?
   B: No, I _____ (not see) her, but I _____ (see) Linda.

4 We _____ (go) to America last summer, but we _____ (not go) to New York.

| 7 |

d) Complete the sentences with some or any.

1 We've got ___some___ food for the party, but we haven't got _____ music!

2 A: Is there _____ fruit here?
   B: Yes, there are _____ apples in the kitchen.

3 I can't watch _____ TV programmes tonight. I've got _____ homework to do.

4 Jenny went shopping with _____ friends yesterday. She bought _____ CDs, but she didn't buy _____ clothes.

| 8 |

e) Replace the underlined words with possessive pronouns.

1 Please give these CDs to Mike. They're his CDs. ___his___

2 These aren't my boots. Harry, are they your boots? _____

3 I don't like their flat, but I love our flat. _____

4 Your jeans are nice. My jeans are horrible! _____

5 Our school is quite small, but their school is very big. _____

6 Your hair is black and her hair is brown. _____

| 5 |

2 Vocabulary

a) Complete the sentences with the words in the box. You will need to use some words twice.

| up | down | in | out | on | off̶ |

1 It's hot in here. I'm going to take ___off___ my jumper.

2 Leo, look at all your books on the floor! Pick them _____ , please.

3 This bag is very heavy. I'm going to put it _____ for a minute.

4 It's cold today. You should put _____ a warm coat.

5 Let's go _____ tonight. I don't want to stay at home.

6 My brother got _____ his car and drove away.

7 Why are you in my room? Please get _____ !

8 Yesterday my cat climbed _____ a tree, and then it couldn't get _____ again!

| 8 |

74   Module 2

b Fill in the puzzle with names of sports. What is the mystery word?

Crossword grid with the letter p *in the shaded mystery column*

1. You do this on a board in snow.
2. You have to jump high to play this game.
3. You need a bike for this sport.
4. You do this in a pool.
5. You do this in the mountains in winter.
6. Ice _____ is a winter team game.
7. You go to the sea with a board for this sport.

[ ] **7**

c Put the letters in order to find the names of jobs.

1. cathree .... *teacher* ....
2. tindest ....
3. crodot ....
4. serun ....
5. lpito ....
6. wrayel ....
7. yescrater ....
8. eerening ....

[ ] **7**

3 Everyday English

Complete the dialogue with the words in the box.

| loads | ~~can't be serious~~ | hardly any |
| saving up | pocket money | one day |

Colin: Hi, Tania. Where are you going?

Tania: To the clothes shop in Spring Street. I work there on Saturdays.

Colin: You work there? You ¹ *can't be serious* ! Why?

Tania: Well, my dad lost his job last month, and he can't give me any ² _____ now.

Colin: Oh, I see.

Tania: So I've got ³ _____ money these days – that's why I work on Saturdays.

Colin: Right.

Tania: I'm in the local cycling team, and I want a new bike. So I'm ⁴ _____ to buy one.

Colin: Good for you!

Tania: Thanks. And you know, I really enjoy working in the shop. I want to have my own shop ⁵ _____ .

Colin: Really? But you need ⁶ _____ of money to open a shop.

Tania: Yes, I know. Oh, Colin, I'm late! I must go. Bye!

Colin: Bye, Tania.

 5

How did you do?

Tick (✓) a box for each section.

Total score [ ] 61	☺ Very good	😐 OK	☹ Not very good
Grammar	25 – 34	19 – 24	less than 19
Vocabulary	17 – 22	13 – 16	less than 13
Everyday English	4 – 5	3	less than 3

Module 3
Far and wide

YOU WILL LEARN ABOUT ...

- The world's best language learners ....
- Holidays in Ireland ....
- An adventure holiday ....
- A science fiction story ....
- Four young mountain climbers ....
- Europeans who went to live in America ....

  ✱ Can you match each picture with a topic?

YOU WILL LEARN HOW TO ...

Speak
- Compare and contrast things
- Compare the lives of famous people
- Talk about your future arrangements
- Talk about your holiday plans
- Make predictions about your future life
- Describe your habits using adverbs
- Re-tell a story

Write
- A letter / An email about a language course
- A magazine article about arrangements for a class trip
- A competition entry about your life in the future
- An email giving advice to a friend

Read
- An article about language learners
- A web page about holidays in Ireland
- A tourist brochure about Ireland
- An article about arrangements for an adventure holiday
- A dialogue from a science fiction story
- An article about climbers in the Himalayas
- An article about Europeans going to live in the USA

Listen
- Teenagers talking about language learning
- A radio interview with a good language learner
- A dialogue about holiday plans
- A dialogue from a science fiction story
- Teenagers making predictions about their future
- A song about an astronaut
- A dialogue about the life of an athlete

Use grammar

Can you match the names of the grammar points with the examples?

Comparative adjectives	It **won't hurt**!
Superlative adjectives	We can't do it – it's **too difficult**.
Present continuous for future arrangements	It's the **longest** river in the world.
will/won't	They stood up **slowly**.
too + adjective	Pronunciation is **more difficult** than grammar.
Adverbs	We**'re visiting** Ireland next summer.

Use vocabulary

Can you think of two more examples for each topic?

Language learning	Future time expressions	Holiday activities	The weather
translate	tomorrow	sightseeing	sunny
have an accent	in two days' time	camping	foggy
....	....	....	....
....	....	....	....

1 Read and listen

a The text is about a group of people. Who are they and why are they special? Read the text quickly to find the answers.

b 🔊 Now read the text again and listen. Mark the statements *T* (true) or *F* (false).

1   A lot of people in Florida speak Spanish as their first language. ☐

2   Some Vaupés River Indians only speak two languages. ☐

3   A Vaupés Indian can't marry someone who speaks the same language. ☐

4   The Vaupés Indians don't have a language that they all understand. ☐

c Do many people in your country speak more than one language? Which languages do people speak?

d One language in the world has more speakers than English. Which do you think it is?

Arabic   Chinese   Russian   Spanish

More than one language

It's not unusual to learn and use more than one language. In many countries around the world, almost everybody speaks more than one language. For example, in some parts of the USA (like Florida), a lot of people speak Spanish as their mother tongue. Most of these people learn English as well, and a lot of English speakers learn Spanish.

But perhaps the world's best language learners are the Indians who live near the Vaupés River in South America. About 10,000 of the Vaupés River Indians live in a small area of the Amazon rainforest. In this area, there are more than 20 completely different languages. All of the Vaupés River Indians speak three languages, often more than three. This is because when a person wants to get married, he or she has to marry someone who speaks a different language. So the children always learn three languages: their mother's first language, their father's first language and also Tukano, the language that all the Vaupés Indians have in common. Then when they are older, they have to marry someone who speaks a different language, and their children have to learn at least three languages. The number is often higher, as the Vaupés people often continue to learn more languages when they are teenagers and adults.

2 Listen

a 🔊 Roberto and Gabriela are talking about the languages they are learning. Listen and read.

b 🔊 Listen again and fill in the names of the languages.

Roberto (from Italy)
First language: Italian
Learning Spanish, German

Gabriela (from Argentina)
First language: Spanish
Learning English, Portuguese

Roberto:
My _____ is good – it's better than my _____ .
Of course, for me _____ is easier than _____ .
That's because it's got a lot of words that are almost the same as _____ . The grammar is very similar, too.

Gabriela:
_____ pronunciation is difficult for me. But of course _____ pronunciation is more difficult! I never know how to pronounce a new word, because the writing and the pronunciation are often very different.

3 Grammar

Comparative adjectives

a Underline examples of comparisons in the texts in Exercise 2. Then complete the table.

	Adjectives	Comparative form
short adjectives (1 syllable)	long	longer
	short	*shorter* ....
	big	bigger
adjectives ending in -*y*	easy	
	happy	happier .... than ...
longer adjectives (2 or more syllables)	difficult	**more** difficult
	important	....
irregular adjectives	bad	worse
	good	....
	far	further

b Complete the comparisons. Choose the correct adjective and use the comparative form.

1 Italian is *more modern than* (old / modern) Latin.
2 The Amazon River is _____ (short / long) the Nile.
3 The Amazon rainforest is _____ (big / small) India.
4 For most Europeans, learning Chinese is _____ (easy / difficult) learning Italian.
5 Sydney is _____ (close to / far from) my country _____ Paris.

4 Pronunciation

than

a 🔊 Listen to the sentences and <u>underline</u> the stressed syllables.

1 Pronunciation is more difficult than grammar.
2 Spanish is easier than German.
3 My speaking is better than my writing.
4 Is French more interesting than English?

b 🔊 How do you pronounce *than*? Listen again and repeat.

5 Speak

Work with a partner. Compare the things in the list. Use adjectives from the box or other adjectives that you know.

interesting	good	beautiful
exciting	friendly	clean
nice	intelligent	easy
important	quiet	boring

1 CD-ROMs / books
2 summer / winter
3 football / tennis
4 dogs / cats
5 cities / villages
6 Spanish / German

6 Listen

a 🔊 Listen to the first part of a radio interview with Matthew Dawson. Fill in the first column of the table with the names of the languages.

b 🔊 Listen again. Tick (✓) where/how Matthew learned each language.

c 🔊 Matthew now talks about how to be a good language learner. Read the ideas in the list. Then listen and tick (✓) the ideas Matthew talks about.

1 Read and listen a lot. ☐

2 Exchange emails or letters with a penfriend who speaks the language. ☐

3 Think of ideas to test yourself when you're learning new words. ☐

4 Listen to cassettes and imitate the pronunciation. ☐

5 Make friends and practise speaking with people who speak the language. ☐

6 Try not to make mistakes, but don't worry about them. ☐

d Which ideas in Exercise 6c do you follow? Which ideas would you like to try?

Language	From his parents	In the country	At school in England	Taught himself
1 *English*	✓			
2 _____				
3 _____				
4 _____				
5 _____				

7 Vocabulary

Language learning

a 🔊 Check that you understand these words about learning and speaking languages. Then listen, check and repeat.

> make mistakes
> imitate   corrects
> translate   look up
> ~~have an accent~~
> means   guess
> communicate

b Read the text. Fill in the spaces with the words/phrases from Exercise 7a.

Advice for language learners

> It can sometimes be a little difficult to learn a foreign language. But there are many things you can do.

When you speak a foreign language, it's normal to ¹ *have an accent* . It's OK – other people can usually understand. It's a good idea to listen to cassettes and try to ² _____ other speakers, to make your pronunciation better.

If you see a new word and you don't know what it ³ _____ , you can sometimes ⁴ _____ the meaning from words you know, or you can ⁵ _____ the word in a dictionary.

A lot of good language learners try not to ⁶ _____ things from their first language. Translation is sometimes a good idea, but try to think in the foreign language if you can!

It's also normal to ⁷ _____ . When your teacher ⁸ _____ a mistake in your writing or speaking, think about it and try to see why it's wrong. But it's more important to ⁹ _____ , so don't be afraid to speak!

8 Grammar
Superlative adjectives

a Read the sentences on the cards. Two of them aren't true. Which do you think they are?

1 The worst language learner lives in England. He started learning French ten years ago, but he can only say 30 French words.

2 The most common word in English is *the*.

3 The easiest language in the world is spoken in Tranquili in Africa. It only has about 1,000 words and there isn't any grammar.

Amazing facts – or just lies?

4 The continent with the most languages is Africa. There are more than 1,000 different languages in Africa.

5 The shortest place names only have one letter. In France there is a place called Y, and U is a place in the Caroline Islands in the Pacific.

6 The best examples of surprising words for *mother* and *father* come from the Georgian language in Central Asia. *Mother* is *deda* and *father* is *mama*.

7 The longest train station name in Britain has got 67 letters. It's a station in Wales called GORSAFAWDDACHAIDRAIGODANHEDDOGLEDDOLLONPENRHYNAREURDRAETHCEREDIGION.

b Cover the text. Can you answer these questions?

1 Which is the continent with the most languages?
2 What are the names of the places with the shortest names?
3 What is the most common word in English?

c Look at the table. Write the adjectives from the box in the second column. Then fill in the comparative and superlative forms.

| difficult | big | happy | fantastic | important |

	Adjectives	Comparative	Superlative
short adjectives (1 syllable)	long short small	longer shorter	longest ....
short adjectives ending in 1 vowel + 1 consonant	.... fat	.... fatter	.... fattest
adjectives ending in -y	easy	easier	....
longer adjectives (2 or more syllables)	frequent	more frequent	most frequent ....
irregular adjectives	bad good many	worse better more	....

d Complete the sentences. Use the superlative form of the adjectives.

1 Many people say that Hungarian is one of the *most difficult* (difficult) languages.
2 When Sarah won $1,000, she was the .... (happy) girl in the world.
3 The Internet was one of the .... (important) inventions in the 1960s.
4 Vatican City is the .... (small) country in the world.
5 When my grandmother died, it was one of the .... (bad) times in my life.
6 The Nile is the .... (long) river in the world.

I have to bounce!

9 Read and listen

a 🔊 Look at the photo story. What do you think *I have to bounce* means? Why do you think Lucy doesn't understand this expression? Read and listen to find the answers.

1

Amy: Bye, Lucy. I have to bounce!

Lucy: What?

Amy: I have to bounce. You know – I have to go. We say that a lot in San Francisco.

2

Lucy: That's cool! What other things do you and your friends say?

Amy: Well, for example, we say someone is 'sketchy' if we think they aren't very nice.

Lucy: Sketchy? All right! I like it.

3

Amy: What about things you say here in Britain?

Lucy: Well, if I say 'He's tasty', do you know what it means?

Amy: Beats me!

Lucy: It means he's good-looking.

4

Amy: Look, there's Dave. He's quite tasty, isn't he?

Lucy: Well, he's a bit sketchy sometimes – but I like him!

Dave: Hi! What are you two laughing about?

Amy: I can't tell you now – I have to bounce!

Dave: Huh?

b Mark the statements *T* (true) or *F* (false).

1 Amy says she has to go. ☐

2 Lucy doesn't like the word *bounce*. ☐

3 A *sketchy* person is someone who is very nice. ☐

4 Amy knows what *tasty* means. ☐

5 In Britain, *tasty* sometimes means 'good-looking'. ☐

10 Everyday English

In all languages, young people invent new words or give words new meanings. Look at the words that young people in Britain used for *good* between 1950 and 2000. What words or phrases are popular with teenagers in your country now?

11 Write

Do one of the two activities.

(a) Write about the languages you speak. Use the texts by Roberto and Gabriela on page 79 to help you.

(b) Imagine you are doing an English course at a language school in Britain or the USA. Write a letter or an email to an English-speaking friend. Think about these questions.

- Where are you writing from? (London? New York? Cambridge?)
- How do you like the English course?
- Who is your teacher?
- How many students are in your class? Where are they from?
- Is your English better now? How? (Is your grammar better? Do you know more words? Do you understand better?)

Start like this:

Dear .... ,

I'm writing to you from [name of place]. *I'm doing an English course here. The course is …*

10 We're going on holiday

✳ Present continuous for future arrangements
✳ Vocabulary: future time expressions, holiday activities

1 Read and listen

a Look at the web page with ideas for a holiday in Ireland. Which ones do you think are good ideas for a holiday?

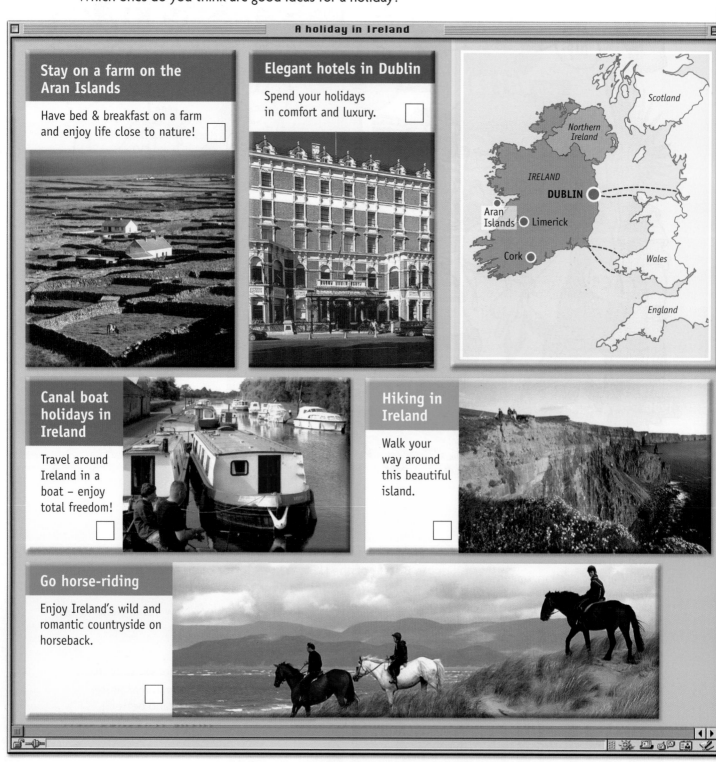

A holiday in Ireland

Stay on a farm on the Aran Islands

Have bed & breakfast on a farm and enjoy life close to nature!

Elegant hotels in Dublin

Spend your holidays in comfort and luxury.

Canal boat holidays in Ireland

Travel around Ireland in a boat – enjoy total freedom!

Hiking in Ireland

Walk your way around this beautiful island.

Go horse-riding

Enjoy Ireland's wild and romantic countryside on horseback.

b 🔊 Listen to Kate and her brother, Greg. They are looking at the web page and planning their family's holiday. Number the activities 1–5 in the order you hear them in the dialogue.

c 🔊 Listen to Kate talking to her friend, Maggie, about the holiday plans. Complete the dialogue.

Maggie: Hey, Kate! How was your weekend?

Kate: Good! My brother and I planned the family summer holiday.

Maggie: Excellent! Where are you going?

Kate: We're ¹_____ to Ireland in August.

Maggie: Oh! How are you ²_____ there?

Kate: We're ³_____ by ferry. And we're ⁴_____ a week on a canal boat on the River Shannon.

Maggie: Great! Are you only ⁵_____ a week in Ireland?

Kate: No, two weeks. After the canal boat, we're ⁶_____ by train to Dublin and we're ⁷_____ in a really nice hotel there for two nights. And then we're ⁸_____ to the Aran Islands. We're ⁹_____ on a farm there.

Maggie: I think you'll have a great holiday! Are all your family ¹⁰_____?

Kate: Yeah. My dad says it's a bit expensive, but he's ¹¹_____ the bank manager tomorrow!

2 Grammar

Present continuous for future arrangements

a Underline examples of the present continuous in the dialogue for Exercise 1c.

We're spending a week on a canal boat.
Dad's seeing the bank manager tomorrow.

> **Rule:** We often use the present continuous to talk about plans and arrangements for the future.

b Complete the sentences.
Use the present continuous form of the verbs.

1 I _____ (visit) my grandparents in Rome next year.

2 Come to our place next Saturday. We _____ (have) a party.

3 Mum _____ (take) my sister to London on Thursday. They _____ (leave) early in the morning.

4 A: _____ you _____ (go) out tonight?
   B: No, I _____ (stay) at home.

5 My brother _____ (not come) on holiday with us this year. He _____ (work) in a shop for six weeks.

6 I've got toothache, so I _____ (see) the dentist tomorrow morning.

3 Vocabulary

Future time expressions

a Here are some expressions we can use to talk about the future. How do you say them in your language?

tomorrow
next week/Saturday/month/ weekend …
in two/five days' time
the day after tomorrow
the week after next

b 🔊 Answer the questions. Then listen and repeat.

1 What day is the day after tomorrow?

   ----

2 What day is it in three days' time?

   ----

3 How many days is it until next Sunday?

   ----

4 What is the month after next?

   ----

4 Speak

Work with a partner. Tell him/her what you're doing:

- this evening
- tomorrow evening
- next Saturday
- next Sunday
- the weekend after next
- next July

A: *This evening I'm staying at home and watching TV.*
B: *I'm going to a restaurant with my parents tomorrow evening.*

5 Read

a What do you know about Ireland? Read the questions and (circle) your answers. If you don't know the answers, guess them.

1 What is the capital of Ireland?

(Dublin) Limerick Cork

2 How many tourists visit Ireland every year?

about 1,000,000
about 2,000,000
about 5,000,000

3 How many people live in Ireland?

3,000,000
5,000,000
10,000,000

4 Which of these pop groups is Irish?

U2 UB40 5ive

b Now read the text. Check your answers to the questions in Exercise 5a.

c Find adjectives in the text to describe these things/ people. Use a dictionary if you need to.

the people:

_warm_____, _____

the country:

_____, _____

the music:

_____

the hotels:

_____

the museums:

_____

Welcome to Ireland
– the perfect place for a holiday

About two million tourists visit the Republic of Ireland every year. They come from all over the world: Europe, Japan, and especially the United States of America, because many Americans have grandparents and great-grandparents who came from Ireland.

Why do so many people come to Ireland? Perhaps it's because the capital city, Dublin, has fascinating museums, comfortable hotels, and great restaurants. Or perhaps it's because the three million people who live in Ireland are so warm and friendly. Maybe it's because it's a charming and very beautiful country. But it's probably because of all of these things.

For young people, Ireland is a great place. Camping is easy, you can go windsurfing and canoeing, cycle around the island, or spend some time on a houseboat on one of the beautiful canals.

The music is exciting too. You can listen to traditional Irish music, or to the many great Irish pop groups. Sometimes, a lucky tourist sees Bono of U2 (the famous Irish band) walking down the street!

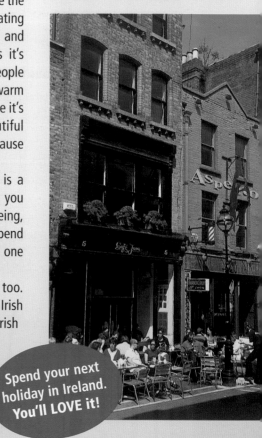

Spend your next holiday in Ireland. **You'll LOVE it!**

6 Vocabulary

Holiday activities

(a) 🔊 Write the names of the activities under the pictures. Then listen, check and repeat.

> canoeing snorkelling horse-riding sailing camping sightseeing windsurfing sunbathing

1 _____

2 _____

3 _____

4 _____

5 _____

6 _____

7 _____

8 _____

(b) Work with a partner. Which of the activities do you like doing on holiday?

A: *I like windsurfing, but I'm not very good at it.*
B: *I don't like sunbathing. It's boring.*

(c) Fill in each space with a verb from the box.

> hire travel stay buy spend

1 _____ souvenirs / presents / postcards / stamps

2 _____ in a hotel / in a bed and breakfast / at a campsite / in a youth hostel / at home

3 _____ to Ireland / by ferry / by car / by plane / by train / by coach

4 _____ your holidays (in Ireland) / some time (on the beach) / two weeks (in Greece)

5 _____ a car / a boat / a bike / a surfboard

7 Speak

Work with a partner. Ask and answer about your plans for your next holiday.

Where / go / for your next holiday?
How / travel / there?   Where / stay?
How much time / spend there?   When / come back?

A: *Where are you going for your next holiday?*
B: *I'm going to …*

8 Pronunciation

/θ/ *(think)* and /ð/ *(that)*

(a) 🔊 Listen and repeat the words.

1 think three month something toothache

2 that those with brother sunbathing

(b) 🔊 Listen and repeat the phrases. <u>Underline</u> *th* when the sound is /θ/. Ⓒircle *th* when the sound is /ð/.

1 Give me those things.

2 There's nothing in my mouth.

3 I think it's Thursday.

4 Your clothes are in the bathroom.

5 My mother thinks I'm crazy.

6 This month we're staying at a youth hostel.

Culture in mind

9 Read

a Where is Paul going for his next holiday? How long is he staying there? Read the text quickly to find the answers.

Adventure holiday in paradise

Paul Roberts (15) lives in New York. Like thousands of other American students, he usually goes away to a summer camp during the school holidays. These camps are just for teenagers, without their parents, and Paul always has a great time. But this summer he's doing something different – he's going on an adventure holiday in Hawaii. He tells us about his arrangements.

'It's a camping holiday for three weeks in Hawaii, for kids from 14 to 18. I'm leaving on 23 July and coming back on 12 August.

First, we're putting on backpacks and hiking through the jungle on an old native Hawaiian trail. They say it's incredibly beautiful, with huge waterfalls and spectacular beaches.

b Now read the text again. Tick the activities that Paul is doing on his holiday.

After this five-day walk, we're staying for two days in a valley on the Pacific Ocean. The main activity here will be surfing. I don't know how to surf, but instructors will teach us how to do it, and I'm really looking forward to this.

Then the organisers are providing mountain bikes and we're going for long rides – about 30 miles a day, around one of Hawaii's volcanoes. And on one day we're meeting a local Hawaiian family and helping them to plant fruit trees on their farm.

After that, we're sailing for three days along the coast, and they say we'll have a chance to swim with dolphins and sea turtles! This sounds fantastic. Finally, we're going out for three days in sea kayaks – we're visiting sea caves and we'll be swimming and snorkelling too.

Every night for the three weeks, we're camping in tents, usually on the beach. This isn't a holiday for couch potatoes! They say you have to be fit, and of course you have to know how to swim and ride a bike. But I think it's going to be a fantastic experience.'

c Mark the statements *T* (true) or *F* (false).

1 Paul usually spends the summer holidays with his parents. ☐

2 His adventure holiday is starting in July. ☐

3 People have to be 15 or older to go on this holiday. ☐

4 First, they are walking for five days. ☐

5 Paul is good at surfing. ☐

6 They are spending some time in a boat. ☐

7 They are sleeping in tents every night. ☐

8 Paul is feeling nervous about the holiday. ☐

d Would you like to go on the adventure holiday to Hawaii? Why / Why not?

10 Write

Imagine your class is going on a school trip for four days. Write an article for your school magazine about your arrangements. Include this information:

● where and when you are going
● which teachers are going
● how you are travelling there (by plane? by ferry? ...)
● where you are staying
● what you are doing there
● how long you are staying and when you are coming back

For your portfolio

What will happen?

* will/won't
* Vocabulary: expressions to talk about the future

1 Read and listen

a Look at the picture of Samantha and Jake. Where are they?

b Read and listen to the dialogue. Why are they frightened?

Samantha: Jake, we went into ¹_____ nearly two years ago and we're still looking for Planet Vulcan. What do you think? Will we find it?

Jake: Oh, yeah. I'm sure we will. Relax, Sam. The ²_____ is a big place, but we've got the computer to help us. We're in a new ³_____ now. Perhaps we'll find it here.

Samantha: OK, but I'm not sure about the computer. I know it's the most powerful computer in the world, but it tells terrible ⁴_____ .

Computer: Good morning, you lucky space travellers! This is your friendly computer speaking. Did you sleep well?

Samantha: Oh, hi, Bob. Yeah, fine, thanks. How about you?

Computer: Excellent! My last night of sleep was excellent.

Jake: Last night of sleep? What do you mean?

Computer: Oh, sorry, guys. Didn't I tell you? That red and blue ⁵_____ out there – can you see it? Our spaceship will ⁶_____ into it in exactly ... um ... one minute from now.

Jake: What? We can't! You have to do something!

Computer: Sorry! I'd like to help, but the ⁷_____ is out of control and there's nothing – I repeat, nothing – I can do. So in 45 seconds, we'll all be dead.

Samantha: Help! Do something!

Computer: I can't. But don't worry. When we die, in exactly ... um ... 30 seconds from now, it'll be very quick and it won't hurt! So I just want to say that I really enjoyed being with you on this spaceship. Thank you for being such good friends! 'We'll meet again, don't know where, don't know when ...'

c ◁»)) Check that you understand all the words in the box. Use them to fill in the spaces. Then listen again and check.

> crash   spaceship   planet   universe   space   jokes   galaxy

d Work with a partner. What do you think will happen? Choose an idea from the box or add your own idea(s).

> I think … they'll die.   Another spaceship will save them.   They'll land safely on the planet.   ? (*your ideas*)

e ◁»)) Listen to the end of the story. What happens? Were you right?

2 Grammar

will/won't

a Look at the examples. Underline examples of *will/'ll* and *won't* in the dialogue in Exercise 1.

> **Will** *we find it?*   *We'**ll** all be dead.*   *It* **won't** *hurt!*

b Complete the table and the rule.

Positive	Negative	Question	Short answers
I/you/we/ they/he/she/ it _____ (will) come	I/you/we/ they/he/she/ it _____ (will not) come	_____ I/you/ we/they/he/ she/it come?	Yes, I/you/we/they/he/ she/it _____ . No, I/you/we/they/he/ she/it _____ (will not).

> **Rule:** We use _____ (*will*) or _____ (*will not*) + base form to make predictions about the future.

c Complete the dialogue with *'ll*, *will* or *won't* and a verb from the box.

> stay   go   find   give   be   get   help

Clara: Oh, Pete, it's the Maths test tomorrow! I hate Maths. I'm sure I ¹ _____ the answers right!

Pete: Don't worry, you ² _____ fine! You got a good result in your last test.

Clara: Yes, but this is more difficult. I really don't feel well. Maybe I ³ _____ to school tomorrow. I ⁴ _____ in bed all day.

Pete: That ⁵ _____ you. The teacher ⁶ _____ you the test on Wednesday.

Clara: You're right. But what can I do?

Pete: Look, why don't I come round to your place this afternoon after school? We can look at the Maths together. You ⁷ _____ it's not so difficult.

Clara: Oh, thanks, Pete.

d Work with a partner. Act out the dialogue in Exercise 2c.

3 Pronunciation

'll

a ◁»)) Listen and tick (✓) the sentence you hear.

1 a I ask the teacher. ☐
   b I'll ask the teacher. ☐
2 a They go to school early. ☐
   b They'll go to school early. ☐
3 a We have a lot of work to do. ☐
   b We'll have a lot of work to do. ☐
4 a I go to London by train. ☐
   b I'll go to London by train. ☐

b Say the b sentences in Exercise 3a.

c Work with a partner. One of you says a sentence from Exercise 3a. The other says which sentence it is.

4 Listen

🔊 Listen to Cristina and Paolo talking about the future, and complete the first two columns of the table. Write ✓ or ✗ for the things they think will or won't happen.

	Cristina	Paolo	Me	My partner
get married	✓			
have children				
go to university				
get a good job				
live abroad				
learn to drive				
become famous				

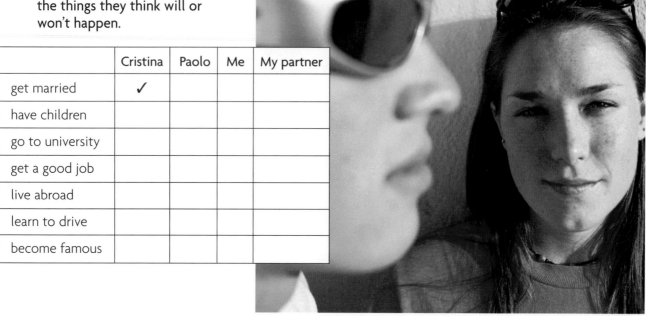

5 Vocabulary

Expressions to talk about the future

(a) Cristina says: *I hope to get a good job.* Does she want to get a good job? Is she sure she'll get one? How do you say *I hope (to)* in your language?

(b) Look at these sentences from the dialogue. Write the <u>underlined</u> phrases in the table.

1   <u>I think I'll</u> get married.
2   <u>I'll probably</u> have two or three children.
3   <u>I don't think I'll</u> live abroad.
4   <u>I doubt I'll</u> be famous.

5   <u>Maybe I'll</u> get married.
6   <u>I'm sure I won't</u> have children.
7   <u>I hope to</u> find a good job.
8   <u>I'm sure I'll</u> learn to drive.

A I believe this will happen	B I believe this won't happen	C I think it's possible that this will happen
I think I'll	....	....

6 Speak

(a) Look at the table in Exercise 4. Complete the third column with your own answers.

(b) Work with a partner. Ask questions and complete the fourth column of the table with your partner's answers.

A: *Will you get married and have children?*   B: *Yes, I'll probably get married and I hope to have children.*

7 Listen

Song

a 🔊 Listen to the song by David Bowie. It's a conversation between an astronaut in space (Major Tom) and someone at the space centre on Earth (Ground Control). Mark each part of the song *A* (Astronaut) or *GC* (Ground Control) to show who is speaking.

b Work with a partner or in a group. Discuss the questions together.

1 Why are the newspapers so interested in Major Tom?
2 What is the 'tin can'?
3 Where is he going when he's 'stepping through the door'?
4 Why is he 'floating'?
5 How do you think he feels?
6 What do you think will happen to him?

c 🔊 Listen again and sing the song.

Space Oddity

1 .... **Ground Control to Major Tom,**
Ground Control to Major Tom,
Take your protein pills and put your helmet on.

2 .... **Ground Control to Major Tom,**
Commencing countdown, engines on.
Check ignition and may God's love be with you.

3 .... **This is Ground Control to Major Tom,**
You've really made the grade
And the papers want to know whose shirts you wear.
Now it's time to leave the capsule, if you dare.

4 .... **This is Major Tom to Ground Control,**
I'm stepping through the door
And I'm floating in a most peculiar way
And the stars look very different today.

[Chorus]

5 .... **For here am I sitting in a tin can, far above the world.**
Planet Earth is blue, and there's nothing I can do.

6 .... **Though I've passed one hundred thousand miles,**
I'm feeling very still.
And I think my spaceship knows which way to go.
Tell my wife I love her very much, she knows.

7 .... **Ground Control to Major Tom,**
Your circuit's dead, there's something wrong.
Can you hear me Major Tom?
Can you hear me Major Tom?
Can you hear me Major Tom?

Astronaut

Ground control

How embarrassing!

8 Read and listen

a 🔊 Look at the photo story and answer the questions. Read and listen to check your answers.

1 What kind of restaurant is this?
2 Is it the beginning or the end of the meal? How do you know?

Waiter: Did you enjoy the meal?
Mum: Yes, it was lovely, thanks.
Waiter: Would you like anything else?
Dad: Just two coffees, please, and the bill.

Waiter: Here you are, sir.
Lucy: Great. This is the best bit of a Chinese meal.
Dad: What? Getting the bill?
Lucy: No, Dad! The cookies!

Lucy: Listen to this. 'Your life will be full of wonderful surprises!'
Mum: Mine says: 'You will have a lot of happiness if you stay happy.' It's nonsense!

Rick: Wow! It says: 'You'll make a journey to an interesting place.' I hope that means we're going to Disneyland for our holiday.
Lucy: Me too. So come on, Dad. What does your fortune cookie say?

Dad: I didn't know it was a fortune cookie. I ate it.
Mum: I don't believe it!
Lucy: Oh, no. How embarrassing!

b Put the sentences in the correct order. Write 1–7 in the boxes.

a ☐ Lucy and Rick are happy when the fortune cookies arrive.

b ☐ Rick says he hopes the family will go to Disneyland.

c [1] Dad asks for coffee and the bill.

d ☐ Dad feels embarrassed.

e ☐ Lucy and her mum read out their fortunes in the fortune cookies

f ☐ Dad eats his fortune cookie.

g ☐ The waiter brings the bill, the coffee and some fortune cookies.

9 Everyday English

a Find the expressions in the photo story. Who says them? How do you say them in your language?

1 Anything else?
2 How embarrassing!
3 This is the best bit.
4 It's nonsense!
5 I don't believe it!

b Read the dialogues. Fill in the spaces with the underlined words in Exercise 9a.

1 **Emma:** I like buying popcorn.
   Robbie: Me too. It's .... about going to the cinema.

2 **Assistant:** There you are, madam. Two kilos of tomatoes.
   ....
   Mrs Shaw: Yes, I'd like a kilo of apples too, please.

3 **John:** Sorry, Mum. I lost my sunglasses.
   Mum: Oh, ... You only bought them three days ago!

4 **George:** I'll be a famous footballer one day.
   Mathilde: Don't talk .... ! You can't kick the ball!

5 **Marina:** I walked into a lamp post while I was coming to school.
   Esra: Really? ....

10 Write

Look at the advertisement. Write about your life in the future for this competition. Use the list of topics and the example to help you.

● Job ● Family ● Money ● Home

In the future I'll go to university and I think I'll become a journalist. I'll probably get married and maybe I'll have two or three children. I hope to have enough money for a good life, but I don't think I'll be very rich. I think I'll have a house near the sea and ...

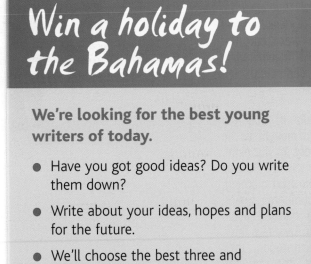

Win a holiday to the Bahamas!

We're looking for the best young writers of today.

● Have you got good ideas? Do you write them down?

● Write about your ideas, hopes and plans for the future.

● We'll choose the best three and publish them.

For your portfolio

12 Never give up!

- ✱ *too* + adjective, adverbs
- ✱ Vocabulary: the weather

1 Read and listen

a Look at the picture. What are the people doing? What dangers are there in this situation?

b Read the text quickly to find the answers to the questions.

1 Who were the people?
2 Where were they?
3 What went wrong?

c Look at the title of the text again. What does *We can't give up* mean?

d 🔊 Now read the text again and listen. Complete the sentences with words from the text.

1 If the weather is very, very cold it's b＿＿＿＿＿ cold. (paragraph 2)
2 If something happens quickly and when you don't expect it, it happens s＿＿＿＿＿ . (paragraph 2)

e Do you think the four young people were brave? Is mountain climbing a sport you'd like to try? Why / Why not?

We can't give up!

Glen Stephens, 24, and his friends, Gaby, 26, Craig, 28, and Tom, 23, are mountain climbers. They work hard in their jobs, but they like to play hard, too. In their free time they travel to other countries and climb some of the world's most dangerous mountains. Their last trip was to the Himalayas in Nepal, to climb one of the highest mountains in the world.

On a day in July, they were in their second week of climbing. They wanted to reach their next camp before it got too dark to climb, so they started early in the morning. The weather was good for a few hours, but suddenly it changed. Snow fell heavily and it was bitterly cold. It was too dangerous to continue.

However, half an hour later, the weather cleared. The four climbers weren't very far from the camp, and they decided to go on.

'Only a few more metres!', Glen said. 'We can't give up now.' They started climbing again, but then there was a loud noise and the snow moved. Avalanche! Suddenly, the four of them were falling. Snow and ice hit their heads while the avalanche threw them 50 metres down the mountain. Luckily, their ropes didn't break, and at last they stopped falling. They stood up slowly. Tom's leg was hurt and Gaby's arms were cut. But they were alive! Together, they started to climb up the mountain again.

'We can't do it! It's too difficult!', Tom thought as he got into his tent for the night. His leg hurt badly and he was exhausted. The next morning, the four climbers talked together, and decided again not to give up. Two days later, on a clear afternoon, they reached the top of the mountain.

2 Grammar

too + adjective

a Match the two parts of the sentences. How do you say the underlined words in your language?

1 The weather was very bad, and it was ...
2 We can't do it! It's ...
3 They wanted to reach the next camp before it ...

a got <u>too dark</u> to climb.
b <u>too dangerous</u> to continue.
c <u>too difficult</u>.

b Complete the sentences.
Use *too* and an adjective from the box.

young	difficult	expensive	short
cold			

1 I can't do this. It's _____ .

2 You can't play.
You're _____ .

€3,000

3 I can't buy it. It's _____ .

4 I'm not swimming today.
The water is _____ .

MOON LIGHT CLUB 18+ ONLY

5 Sorry, you can't go in. You're _____ .

c Complete the sentences. Use the words in the box.

very old	too old	very big	too big
very heavy	too heavy		

1 Look at that house. It's _____ .
2 I think this hat is _____ .
3 I can't lift it. It's _____ .
4 These bags are _____ .
5 These paintings are _____ .
6 We can't use this phone now. It's _____ .

3 Vocabulary

The weather

a 🔊 Match the sentences with the pictures. Write 1–4 in the boxes. Then listen, check and repeat.

1   It's hot today.   2   It's warm today.
3   It's cool today.   4   It's cold today.

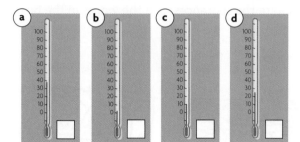

b What's the weather like? Use the words in the box.

sunny   cloudy   windy   foggy
snowing   raining

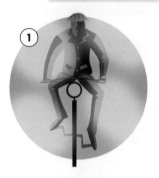

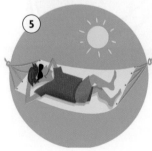

1   It's   4   It's ....
2   It's   5   It's ....
3   It's   6   It's ....

4 Grammar

Adverbs

a Look at the examples from the text on page 96 and complete the rule.

*It was **bitterly** cold.*   *His leg hurt **badly**.*
*Snow fell **heavily**.*   *They work **hard** in their jobs.*

> **Rule:** Adverbs describe adjectives and ....
> To form a regular adverb, we usually add ....
> to the adjective. If the adjective ends with *y*,
> change the *y* to .... before adding ....

b Underline more examples of adverbs in the text on page 96.

c Complete the tables.

Adjectives	Regular adverbs
slow	*slowly*
bad	....
loud	....
quiet	....
lucky	....
easy	....

Adjectives	Irregular adverbs
fast	*fast*
good	*well*
early	....
late	*late*
hard	....

d Complete the sentences. Use adverbs from the tables in Exercise 4c.

1   I play the piano very *badly* , but I can sing quite ....
2   She talks very .... It's often difficult to hear her.
3   They missed the train because they arrived .... at the station.
4   My English isn't very good. Can you speak more ...., please?
5   If you want to pass your exam, you need to study ....

5 Speak

a Work with a partner. Ask and answer the questions.

1   Do you get up early or late?
2   Do you eat quickly or slowly?
3   Do you usually work hard?

b Tell your partner about other things you do. Use the adverbs in the box.

quickly   slowly   well   badly   loudly   quietly

A: *I can speak French quite well.*
B: *I write quickly, but I read slowly.*

6 Pronunciation

/əʊ/ (go)

a 🔊 Listen and repeat the words.

show   no   clothes
rope   <u>home</u>work
house<u>boat</u>   <u>snow</u>ing

b 🔊 Listen to the sentences. <u>Underline</u> the words or syllables that have the /əʊ/ sound. Then listen again, check and repeat.

1 Only a few more metres!
2 They stood up slowly.
3 They decided to go on.
4 The snow was bitterly cold.
5 Sorry! I broke the window.
6 **A:** Who's on the phone?
    B: I don't know.

7 Listen

a Amy has to find out about a sportsperson for homework. Her mother tells her about an athlete called Wilma Rudolph.

Before you listen, look at the pictures about Wilma's life. Work with a partner and put the pictures in order. Write 1–8 in the boxes.

a    **b**    **c**    **d**

e    **f**    **g**    **h**

b 🔊 Listen to Amy and her mother talking about Wilma Rudolph. Check your answers.

c 🔊 Listen again. Under each picture write the year or Wilma's age.

8 Speak

Work with a partner. Together, tell the story of Wilma Rudolph in your own words. Use the pictures to help you. Start like this:

Wilma Rudolph was a famous American athlete. She was born ...

Culture in mind

9 Read

a Look at the photos. When and where do you think they were taken? Who were the people in the photos? Read the text quickly to check your ideas.

b Now read the text again. Then (circle) the correct answers.

1 .... were two countries which sent a lot of immigrants to the USA.
   a Ireland and Europe
   b Italy and Ireland
   c East Europe and Germany

2 Most of the immigrants lived ....
   a in cities   b on farms
   c in houses

3 It wasn't hard to ....
   a find work
   b get a lot of money
   c be successful

4 When they first arrived, a lot of the men worked as ....
   a engineers   b builders
   c politicians

5 These people were very ....
   a unhappy   b rich
   c determined

6 President Kennedy said that American life was .... because of immigration.
   a better   b worse   c difficult

c Find words in the text with these meanings.

1 period of 100 years (paragraph 1)
   ----

2 went back (paragraph 2)
   ----

3 people who arrived a short time ago (paragraph 3)
   ----

4 flats (paragraph 3)
   ----

5 using their hands (paragraph 3)
   ----

6 very tall city buildings (paragraph 3)

New Americans

At the end of the 19th century, thousands of people left Europe to come to the USA. They came to find jobs and new opportunities in the 'new world'. First there were Irish and German migrants, then Italians and East Europeans as well. Between 1890 and 1920, about 18 million people arrived in the USA.

Most of these migrants came with very little money. Some went to the country and worked on small farms, but usually they lived in the cities, where jobs were easy to find. Some people found the new life too strange and difficult and returned to their home country. But most of them were determined to succeed in the USA.

Life was hard. Americans often looked down on the newcomers. Families shared small apartments in crowded buildings. Women often worked at home, making clothes for very little pay. A lot of the men took jobs as manual workers. They made railways, bridges and roads, and built the first skyscrapers. They worked hard and saved carefully, and they often sent money back to their families in their home country.

Gradually, they became successful in their new home. Families started shops, restaurants and other businesses and these soon grew larger.

European migrants also had great success in music and the new field of film-making. They succeeded in business, sports and politics. By the 1960s, President John F. Kennedy could say, 'Everywhere immigrants have enriched and strengthened the fabric of American life.'

Today, a huge new wave of migration is coming to the USA from Asia and Latin America. These people face the same kinds of difficulties – and they share the same determination to succeed.

10 Write

(a) Imagine you got this email from your friend, Spiros, who is studying English in a language school. Why is he unhappy?

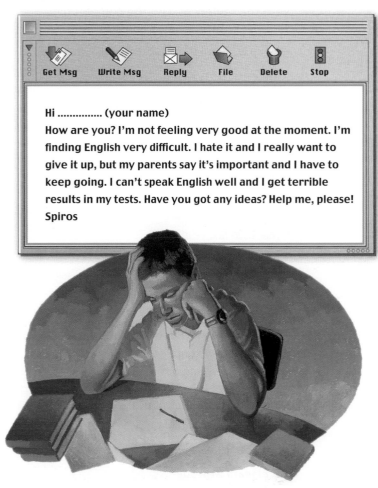

> Hi .... (your name)
> How are you? I'm not feeling very good at the moment. I'm finding English very difficult. I hate it and I really want to give it up, but my parents say it's important and I have to keep going. I can't speak English well and I get terrible results in my tests. Have you got any ideas? Help me, please!
> Spiros

(b) Complete the email reply to Spiros. Give him some ideas about learning English. Use some of these phrases.

> I think it's a good idea to ...
> Try to ...   Remember to ...
> Why don't you ...?
> ... is good/useful/helpful, because ...
> ... will help you to ...

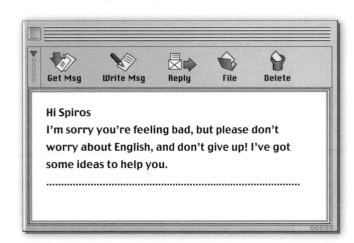

> Hi Spiros
> I'm sorry you're feeling bad, but please don't worry about English, and don't give up! I've got some ideas to help you.
> ....

For your portfolio

1 Grammar

a Complete the sentences. Use the comparative or superlative form of the adjectives.

1 Today is the __longest__ (long) day of the year.
2 For me, Geography is .... (difficult) than Maths.
3 History is the .... (easy) subject at school.
4 I feel dreadful! This is the .... (bad) day of my life!
5 I don't argue with Joe, because he's .... (big) than me.
6 Sally is .... (good) than me at Art.
7 I think my results will be .... (bad) this year than last year.
8 If you want to be fit, a healthy diet and lots of exercise are the .... (important) things.

☐ 7

b Look at Linda's diary.
Write sentences about the things she's doing next weekend.

> **Saturday**
>
> 10.00 driving lesson
>
> 3.00 meet Gerard in café
>
> 6.00 cinema with Sue
>
> **Sunday**
>
> 12.30 lunch with Wendy
>
> 5.00 homework
>
> 7.30 cousins arrive from Canada!

Saturday
1 At 10.00 she _'s having a driving lesson._
2 At 3.00 she ....
3 At 6.00 she and Sue ....
Sunday
4 At 12.30 she and Wendy ....
5 At 5.00 ....
6 At 7.30 ....

☐ 5

c Complete the sentences.
Use the verbs with *will* or *won't*.

1 My train is running late, so I __won't be__ (be) home before 7 o'clock.
2 Julie isn't feeling well. I think she .... (stay) in bed this morning.
3 He's a really good actor. I'm sure he .... (become) famous one day.
4 We can go to the beach tomorrow. I'm sure it .... (rain).
5 What do you think? .... you .... (go) to university?
6 James went to London today, so he .... (be) at the party tonight. ☐ 5

d ⵔ Circle the correct words.

1 My parents are ⓐ angry / angrily because I didn't do the washing-up.
2 Our team lost yesterday. Everyone played *bad / badly*.
3 Last week's test was *easy / easily*.
4 My sister sings *good / well*.
5 Hurry up, Jill! Why are you walking so *slow / slowly*?
6 Last night I heard a *loud / loudly* noise outside my room.
7 It was a *slow / slowly* journey and we arrived very *late / lately*. ☐ 7

2 Vocabulary

a Complete the sentences with the words in the box.

> imitate translate make mistakes look up
> accent mean guess communicate

1 When I speak English, I sometimes __make mistakes__ in grammar, but I can still .... with English speakers.
2 Excuse me, what does this word .... ?
3 I want my pronunciation to be better, so I listen to cassettes and .... the speakers.
4 For homework, our teacher sometimes gives us texts in English and we have to .... them into our language.
5 My father speaks good English, but he has a very strong ....
6 When I don't know a word, I try to .... the meaning. If I can't do that, I .... the word in my dictionary.

☐ 7

b Write the holiday activities in the lists.

> ~~swimming~~   windsurfing   camping
> horse-riding   sightseeing   snorkelling
> canoeing   cycling   sunbathing   sailing

in/on water	not in/on water
swimming	

☐ **9**

c Fill in the crossword with words to describe the weather.

1 s	n	o	2 w	i	n	g		3
					4			
		5						
			6					
	7							
8								

1 ➡ Look! It's .... The garden is white.

1 ⬇ It's .... outside. I'm going to sunbathe on the beach.

2   18° – it's .... today.

3   It's too .... to drive. We can't see the road in front of us.

4   It was very .... yesterday. A tree fell down in my street.

5   Take an umbrella. It's .... now.

6   It was .... yesterday. The temperature was 34°.

7 ➡ It's .... today. We can't see the sun.

7 ⬇ Come out of the sun. It's nice and .... under the trees.

8   Last night it was −10°. That's very .... !

☐ **9**

Everyday English

Complete the dialogue with the words in the box.

> embarrassing   the best bit
> anything else   nonsense   ~~cool~~
> believe it

Lucy: A funny thing happened last week.

Teresa: What?

Lucy: Well, we went to a Chinese restaurant for a meal, and then we had fortune cookies.

Teresa: Oh, I love those.

Lucy: Me too. Mine said, 'Your life will be full of wonderful surprises!'

Teresa: Wow! That's [1] ___*cool*___ !

Lucy: Mum got a strange one. It said, 'You will have a lot of happiness if you stay happy.'

Teresa: Well, that's [2] _____ ! It doesn't mean anything.

Lucy: Yes, I know. But [3] _____ was when my dad ate his fortune cookie with the paper inside.

Teresa: Oh, no! I don't [4] _____ !

Lucy: It's true! It was really [5] _____ ! There were loads of people in the restaurant, and they all laughed.

Teresa: Did [6] _____ happen?

Lucy: No, we paid the bill and left after that.

☐ **5**

How did you do?

Tick (✓) a box for each section.

Total score	Very good	😐 OK	☹ Not very good
☐ **54**			
Grammar	18 – 24	13 – 17	less than 13
Vocabulary	18 – 25	14 – 17	less than 14
Everyday English	4 – 5	3	less than 3

Module 4
The things people do!

YOU WILL LEARN ABOUT ...

- New Year celebrations and resolutions ....
- Different cultures ....
- Tips for tourists in Britain ....
- A meeting with a gorilla ....
- Amazing records ....
- The fans of Elvis Presley ....

* Can you match each picture with a topic?

YOU WILL LEARN HOW TO ...

Speak
- Talk about your future intentions
- Give advice and recommendations
- Describe what things are / were like
- Talk about future possibilities
- Tell a story about a brave person
- Talk about experiences in your life

Write
- An email about your last New Year's Eve
- A letter / An email giving tips about your country
- The story of a film or a book
- A letter / An email about a visit to Los Angeles

Read
- A short text about New Year
- A dialogue about obligations
- A quiz about customs in different countries
- A brochure giving tourist tips about Britain
- A story about gorillas
- Short texts about amazing record-breakers
- An article about one of these record-breakers
- An article about the fans of Elvis Presley

Listen
- A dialogue about New Year's resolutions
- A dialogue about a teenager's unlucky day
- Short dialogues about customs in different countries
- A dialogue about bravery and risk
- An interview about strange pets

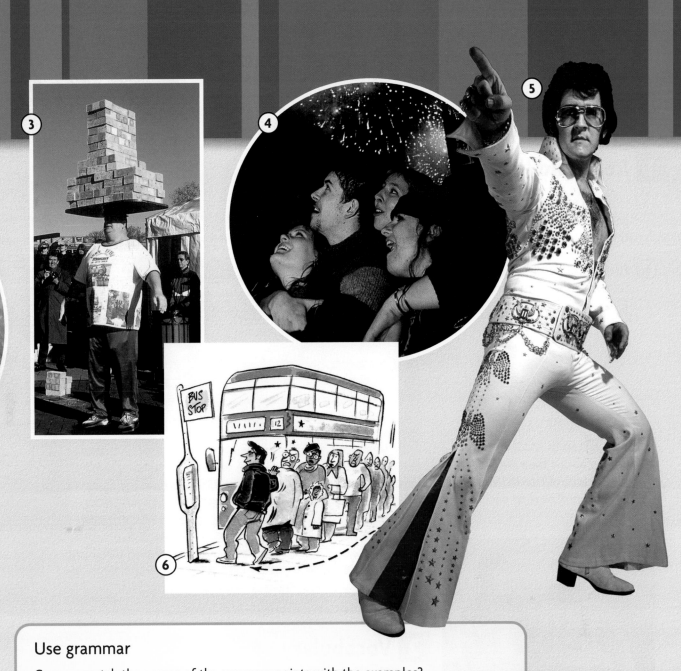

Use grammar

Can you match the names of the grammar points with the examples?

be going to	You **must** remember to feed the dog.
must/mustn't	**I've never been** to Paris.
should/shouldn't	**I'm going to** get fit.
What's it like?	If I **don't move**, he'll **go** away.
First conditional	What's the new girl **like**?
Present perfect + *ever/never*	You **shouldn't** arrive late.

Use vocabulary

Can you think of two more examples for each topic?

Phrasal verbs	Personality adjectives	Opinion adjectives	Animals
take up	hard-working	fantastic	rabbit
throw away	friendly	awful	snake
....	....	....	....
....	....	....	....

13 Good intentions

✱ *be going to* (intentions and predictions), *must/mustn't*
✱ Vocabulary: phrasal verbs (2)

1 Read and listen

a How do British people celebrate New Year? Read the text to check your ideas.

b Find words or phrases in the text with these meanings.

1 the day before 1 January

....

2 12 o'clock at night

....

3 the time when it starts to get light in the morning

....

c 🔊 Listen to Mark and Annie talking about their New Year's resolutions. Write *M* (Mark), or *A* (Annie) next to each resolution.

Mark   Annie

1 I'm going to be more healthy. ☐

2 I'm going to take up scuba diving. ☐

3 I'm going to be more organised. ☐

4 I'm not going to eat chocolate. ☐

5 I'm not going to have arguments with my sister. ☐

6 I'm going to eat fruit every day. ☐

New Year's resolutions

It's 31 December – New Year's Eve. All over Britain, people are having parties, sometimes in their homes, sometimes out in the street. Ten seconds before midnight, the countdown begins: 10–9–8–7–6–5–4–3–2–1 ... *Happy New Year!* Fireworks go off, and people kiss and stand in a circle to sing the old Scottish song *Auld Lang Syne*. They often keep up the celebrations until dawn.

Also at this time, people often begin to think about the year that is just starting. They think about the changes they're going to make and the things they're going to do in the new year. They make promises to themselves, called New Year's resolutions. But of course, people don't always stick to their resolutions!

2 Vocabulary

Phrasal verbs (2)

a 🔊 Match the verbs with the definitions. Then listen and repeat.

1 **take up** scuba diving   a put in the rubbish bin

2 **give up** chocolate   b start to do or learn

3 **throw away** my old papers   c continue

4 **work out** our problems   d stop doing something you enjoy

5 **keep** it **up**   e discover answers for

b Complete the sentences. Use the correct form of the phrasal verbs in Exercise 2a.

1 Last year my dad *gave up* smoking. He's a lot healthier now.

2 The Maths test was difficult, but I think I .... most of the answers.

3 Caroline loves sport. Three months ago she .... tennis and she's already very good at it.

4 I'm studying much harder now and I'm getting good results. I hope I can .... it .... !

5 Our old radio didn't work, so we .... it ....

3 Grammar

be going to: intentions

a Read the rule and complete the table.

Positive	Negative	Questions	Short answers
I'm (am) going to change	I'm not (am not) going to change	Am I going to change?	Yes, I .... No, I'm not.
you/we/they 're (are) going to change	you/we/they .... (are not) going to change	.... you/we/they going to change?	Yes, you/we/they .... No, you/we/they aren't.
he/she/it 's (is) going to change	he/she/it .... (is not) going to change	.... he/she/it going to change?	Yes, he/she/it is. No, he/she/it ....

b Complete the sentences. Use the words in the box with the correct form of *be going to*.

> work out their problems   not eat unhealthy food
> ~~make some changes in their lives~~   not be untidy
> stop arguing with your sister   throw away her rubbish

1 Mark and Annie *are going to make some changes in their lives* .
2 Annie's room ....
3 Annie and her sister ....
4 Annie ....
5 Mark ....
6 **Mark:** .... you .... ?
   Annie: Yes, I ....

be going to: predictions

c Read the rule. Then complete the sentences with *be going to* and the verb in brackets.

1 There isn't a cloud in the sky. It's *going to be* (be) sunny tomorrow.
2 The river is deep here. It .... (not be) easy to get across.
3 I know they like modern art. They .... (love) this painting.
4 It's 8.40, Steve! You .... (be) late!
5 Angela .... (not get) good results this year. She hardly ever studies at home.
6 .... we .... (win) the match?

d Match the sentences with the pictures. Write 1–6 in the boxes.

1 He's going to fall off!
2 I'm going to wear this tonight!
3 It's going to rain.
4 We aren't going to do any work this afternoon.
5 This is going to be difficult.
6 I'm going to have a shower.

e Which of the sentences in Exercise 3d are intentions? Which are predictions?

4 Speak

a Work with a partner. Find out about his/her intentions for:

- this evening
- next weekend
- his/her next holiday

b Work with another partner. Say what your first partner is going to do.

This evening, Maria's going to do her homework. Next weekend, she's going to …

5 Read and listen

a 🔊 Simon's parents are going to London for a day. Look at the first picture. What do you think Simon's mother wants him to do? Read and listen to check your ideas.

Mum: Now don't forget, Simon, I want you to do two things, OK? You mustn't forget to post this letter – it's very important.

Simon: Don't worry, Mum. I'm going to take it to the post office in half an hour.

Mum: And the dog. You must remember to feed her.

Simon: I know, I know. Don't worry. You and Dad go off now and have a good time.

Mum: Right, we must go. It's late and we mustn't miss the train. Oh, but look at this washing-up. I'll just do it quickly before we go.

Simon: No, Mum. I'll do the washing-up. It's no problem.

Dad: Come on, Janet!

Mum: Right then. See you soon.

Simon: Bye, Mum.

b 🔊 When Simon's mother comes home, she isn't very happy. Look at the second picture and answer the questions. Then listen to check your ideas.

1 What is Simon's mother going to say?
2 Why do you think Simon didn't do the things she asked him to do?

c 🔊 Listen again and put the sentences in the correct order. Write 1–7 in the boxes.

a ☐ He called an ambulance.
b ☐ He couldn't get into the house because the key was inside.
c ☐ He cycled to his grandmother's house.
d ☐ He heard Mr Smith calling for help.
e ☐ Simon left the house to post the letter.
f ☐ He went back to the house to get some money.
g ☐ He went to help Mr Smith.

d Have you ever had an unlucky day? Tell the class what happened.

6 Grammar

must/mustn't

a Look at the examples. Then complete the rule and the table.

*You **must** remember to feed the dog.*
*You **mustn't** forget to post this letter.*

> **Rule:** We use .... when we want to say that it's important to do something. We use .... when we want to say that it's important *not* to do something.

Positive	Negative
I/you/we/they/he/she/it .... go	I/you/we/they/he/she/it .... (**must not**) go

b Look at the pictures and complete the sentences. Use *must* or *mustn't* and a verb from the box.

> touch   say   practise   listen   ~~be~~   miss

7 Pronunciation

must & mustn't

a 🔊 *Must* is usually stressed, and sometimes the stress is very strong. Listen and repeat. Which sentences put a strong stress on *must*? Why, do you think?

I must go to the post office later.
You must work harder.
You must come to my party!
We must go home now.

b 🔊 Listen to these sentences. Notice the pronunciation of *mustn't*: /mʌsənt/. Listen again and repeat.

You mustn't eat that!
We mustn't forget.
You mustn't drive too fast.
I mustn't be late.

c 🔊 Say the sentences from Exercise 6b. Listen and check.

1

I _mustn't be_ late for school.

2

You .... more often.

3

We .... the beginning of the film.

4

I .... anything stupid!

5

You .... it.

6

You .... to this CD – it's great!

A birthday party

8 Read and listen

a 🔊 Look at the photo story. There are two things that Lucy is not very happy about. What are they? Read and listen to check your answers.

1

Mum: So, Lucy, next week you're going to be 16! What about a party here at home?
Lucy: Really, Mum? Can I?
Mum: Of course.
Lucy: Great! I'm going to invite everyone!

2

Mum: OK. I'll make a birthday cake and Dad will do a barbecue in the garden.
Lucy: Oh. You mean ... you and Dad are going to be here?
Mum: Of course. Why? What's the problem?
Lucy: Well ... you know. All my friends are going to be here ...

Later that day ...

3

Mum: Listen, I was thinking about your party and I've got another idea. Dad and I will go out for the evening. I'll cook the food for your party before we go.
Lucy: Mum, that's brilliant. Thank you.

4

Mum: Yes, we'll go to the cinema. So we'll be back at about 10.30, OK?
Lucy: 10.30? That early?
Mum: Well, you know your father has to get up early for work. The party can't go on all night.
Lucy: Yeah, I know, Mum, but ... 10.30?

b Match the two parts of each sentence. Then put the sentences in the right order. Write 1–6 in the boxes.

a	☐ Lucy's parents want to come home	to have a barbecue at home.
b	☐ Lucy isn't happy because	to go out for the evening.
c	☐ Lucy is going to be	too early for the end of the party.
d	☐ Her parents decide	at 10.30 in the evening.
e	☐ Her mother's first idea for a party is	16 next week.
f	☐ Lucy thinks 10.30 is	she doesn't want her parents to be at the party.

9 Everyday English

a) We often use *I'll* + base form of the verb to make offers of help. Look at these
sentences from the unit. Who said them, and who were they speaking to?

1   *I'll **do** the washing-up.*
2   *I'll **make** a birthday cake.*
3   *I'll **cook** the food for your party before we go.*

b) Match the sentences.

1   Kate doesn't eat meat.
2   Oh, no. I've forgotten my money.
3   I'm really angry with Maria.
4   I need to talk to Eva, but I haven't got her phone number.
5   I'm so disappointed I can't watch the match.
6   Oh, no! The phone's ringing again!

a   I'll give it to you. It's here in my book.
b   I can understand why. I'll talk to her.
c   No problem. I'll cook a vegetarian meal.
d   Don't worry. I'll answer it.
e   That's OK. I'll pay for both of us.
f   I've got a video recorder. I'll record it for you.

c) Write what these people are saying. Use the verbs in the box.

| help   pay   answer   fix |

1 _____ it.
2 _____ it for you.
3 _____ you.
4 _____ for your ticket.

10 Write

Imagine it's 1 January and
you get this email from
your Scottish friend,
Jessie.

Write an email in reply
to Jessie. Tell her about:

● your New Year's Eve
● your New Year's
  resolution(s) and a
  resolution made by
  someone in your
  family
● what you're going
  to do this week

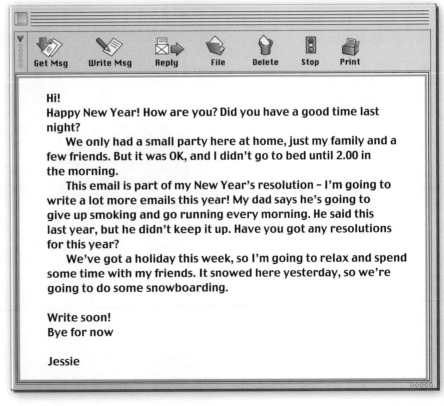

Hi!
Happy New Year! How are you? Did you have a good time last
night?
    We only had a small party here at home, just my family and a
few friends. But it was OK, and I didn't go to bed until 2.00 in
the morning.
    This email is part of my New Year's resolution – I'm going to
write a lot more emails this year! My dad says he's going to
give up smoking and go running every morning. He said this
last year, but he didn't keep it up. Have you got any resolutions
for this year?
    We've got a holiday this week, so I'm going to relax and spend
some time with my friends. It snowed here yesterday, so we're
going to do some snowboarding.

Write soon!
Bye for now

Jessie

For your portfolio

(14) You shouldn't do that!

✱ *should/shouldn't, What's it like?*
✱ Vocabulary: personality adjectives, adjectives for expressing opinions

1 Read and listen

(a) Check that you know the meanings of these words. Match them with the pictures.

1 to bow   2 present   3 pocket   4 cow   5 leather
6 the top of your head

(b) Look at the quiz. Which country do you think matches each custom (1–8)? Write a–h in the boxes.

(c) 🔊 Listen to the dialogues and check your answers to the quiz.

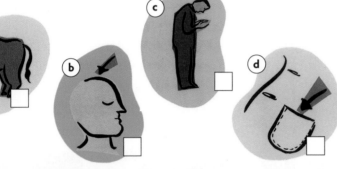

QUIZ: What do you know about other cultures?

Can you match the countries with these customs?

1. Students bow to their teacher when he or she comes into the room.

2. You shouldn't give someone a clock as a present.

3. You shouldn't give someone a toy dog or a card with a picture of a dog.

4. You shouldn't cross your arms when you're talking to someone.

5. When you go to someone's house for dinner, it is polite to arrive five or ten minutes late.

6. When you go to someone's house, you should arrive on time.

7. You shouldn't touch the top of someone's head.

8. You shouldn't give someone a present made of cow's leather.

a Germany
b China
c England
d Saudi Arabia
e Japan
f Thailand
g Turkey
h India

2 Grammar

should/shouldn't

a Look at the examples and read the rule. <u>Underline</u> examples of *should* and *shouldn't* in the quiz.

*When you go to someone's house, you **should** arrive on time.*
*You **shouldn't** give someone a clock as a present.*

> **Rule:** We use *should* or *shouldn't* to say 'It's a good idea' or 'It isn't a good idea'.

b Complete the table.

Positive	Negative	Questions	Short answers
I/you/we/they/he/she/it **should** go	I/you/we/they/he/she/it _____ **(should not)** go	**Should** I/you/we/they/he/she/it go?	Yes, I/you/we/they/he/she/it _____ . No, I/you/we/they/he/she/it _____ **(should not)**.

c Complete the dialogues. Use *should* or *shouldn't* and a verb from the box.

> go   watch   wear

1 **Steve:** I don't know which jacket to wear.
   Paul: The white one's great. I think you ~~should wear~~ that one.

2 **Jane:** There's a programme about Japan on TV tonight.
   Tim: Really? Then I _____ it. I'm doing a project on Japan.

3 **Alex:** My eyes really hurt. _____ I _____ to the doctor?
   Father: No, but you _____ television so much, Alex.

4 **Amy:** I'm tired.
   Lucy: Me too. It's nearly 11.30. I think we _____ to bed.

5 **Anna:** What do you think? _____ I _____ jeans to the party this evening?
   Carol: No, everybody's wearing party clothes. You _____ your long dress.

6 **Peter:** Mum, I feel awful this morning.
   Mother: Yes, you look ill. Perhaps you _____ to school today.

3 Speak

Work with a partner.
Student A: Read the role card below.
Student B: Turn to page 137 and read the role card.
Take it in turns to listen to your partner's problem and give advice with *should* or *shouldn't*.

> **Student A**
>
> You play the guitar in a band. You practise for about two hours every evening, so you don't have time to do all your schoolwork. Your parents are unhappy because your test results are bad. They want you to leave the band and do your schoolwork. You are very unhappy because you love playing in the band, but you want to get good school results too. Should you stay in the band? Should you leave? Ask Student B.

4 Vocabulary
Personality adjectives

a 🔊 Listen and repeat the adjectives.

kind hard-working polite honest organised
cheerful relaxed friendly

b Complete the sentences with the adjectives in Exercise 4a.

1 A .... person is usually happy and smiles a lot.

2 An .... person tells you what he/she really thinks.

3 A .... person doesn't worry about things.

4 A .... person works a lot.

5 An .... person is tidy and keeps things in order.

6 A .... person helps people and thinks about their feelings.

7 A .... person is easy to talk to and makes friends easily.

8 A .... person always says *please* and *thank you*.

c 🔊 Write the adjectives under the pictures. Then listen, check and repeat.

unfriendly dishonest unkind lazy miserable
nervous rude disorganised

d Complete the table of opposites.

Adjectives	Opposites
1 kind	....
2 cheerful	....
3 polite	....
4 honest	....
5 organised	....
6 relaxed	....
7 hard-working	....
8 friendly	....

e Complete the sentences with adjectives. Use your own ideas.

1 I think I'm a/an .... person.

2 My best friend is .... and ....

3 Our neighbours are very ....

4 I don't like people who are ....

1 ....

2 ....

3 ....

4 ....

5 ....

6 ....

7 ....

8 ....

5 Pronunciation

Silent consonants

(a) 🔊 Listen and repeat the words. In each word, there is a 'silent' consonant which we don't pronounce. Underline the silent consonants.

1 honest   2 should   3 school
4 write   5 climb   6 know   7 two

(b) 🔊 Which consonants are silent in these words? Listen, check and repeat.

1 shouldn't   2 Thailand   3 foreign
4 listen   5 island   6 fascinating

(c) 🔊 Listen and repeat the sentences.

1 They should go to school.
2 I speak two foreign languages.
3 I know he's an honest person.
4 It's a fascinating island.
5 You shouldn't climb on the wall.

6 Grammar

What's it like?

(a) Match the questions with the answers.

1 What was the weather like on your holiday? ☐
2 What's your new teacher like? ☐
3 What are the people like in New York? ☐
4 What were the films like last night? ☐
5 What's this CD like? ☐

a They're very friendly and helpful.
b It's brilliant! You should listen to it.
c Well, I thought they were a bit boring.
d Awful! It rained all the time.
e She's nice and she's really funny!

(b) When we ask for an opinion about something or someone, we can ask: *What + be + subject + like?* Look at the questions in Exercise 6a and complete the table.

What	is ------- ------- were	he / .... / it they	.... ?

c Write the questions. Use the words in brackets.

1 A: I went to Greece last year.
   B: Really? What ___was it like___ ? (it)
2 A: I've got the new Oasis CD.
   B: Oh? What _____? (it)
3 A: There's a new girl in our class.
   B: A new girl? What _____? (she)
4 A: We visited Spain a few weeks ago.
   B: Oh, that's nice! What _____?
   (the weather)
5 A: I've got some new trainers.
   B: Really? What _____? (they)
6 A: I read three books last week.
   B: Wow! What _____? (they)

7 Vocabulary

Adjectives for expressing opinions

(a) 🔊 Here are some adjectives we can use to give an opinion. Write them in the columns. Then listen, check and repeat.

~~boring~~   ~~brilliant~~   interesting   attractive
fantastic   awful   cool   dull   ugly   dreadful

+	−
brilliant	boring

(b) Which adjectives from Exercise 7a can you use to describe:

1 a film?   3 a city/town?   5 the weather?
2 a person?   4 a party?

8 Speak

Work with a partner. Ask and answer questions about the things in the box.

> your brother/sister/parents/boyfriend/girlfriend
> your town or city   your home   your last holiday
> your favourite singer   your last weekend

A: *What's your brother like?*
B: *He's OK sometimes. He's ...*

Culture in mind

9 Read

a Look at the title and the first two paragraphs of the text. What do you think the word *tips* means?

b Read the text. Match paragraphs 1–5 with the pictures. Write 1–5 in the boxes.

c Now read the text again. Then look at pictures a–e. Write sentences to explain what the people should and shouldn't do in Britain.

    a *She should look to the right.*

d Which of the things in the text are also true in your country?

Tips for the tourist in Britain

When you travel to a foreign country, you can see that the customs of the people there aren't always the same as yours. So before you go abroad, it's a good idea to find out something about the people who live in the country you're visiting.

The British are generally helpful and friendly but there are some things you should remember, so you don't make mistakes.

1 At bus stops, in cinemas and in shops, the British usually stand in queues. You shouldn't go to the front – you should stand in the queue and wait, like everyone else.

2 British people are usually polite and say *please* and *thank you* a lot. So when you're hungry, for example, you shouldn't say *I want a sandwich*. You should say *Can I have a sandwich, please?* When someone says *Thank you*, you can reply *You're welcome*.

3 When people say things you don't understand, you should say *Sorry?* or *Pardon?* and ask them to say it again. You shouldn't say *What?* – it isn't polite.

4 In some countries, people often kiss each other on the cheek when they meet. In Britain, you should only do this with people who are your friends or relatives. In formal situations, you should shake hands with the person.

5 Finally, don't forget – the British drive on the left. So before you cross the road, you should always look to the right!

10 Write

a Jill's penfriend, Mathilde, is visiting Britain in March. Read Jill's letter and match the topics with the paragraphs.

a Things that Mathilde should/shouldn't do in Britain ☐

b Things that Mathilde should take to Britain ☐

c British people ☐

e Work with a partner. Make a list of useful tips for British tourists who are coming to visit your country.

I WANT THE SUGAR.

Hi Mathilde

I'm really happy you're coming to visit us here in Britain. I'm writing to tell you some things about my country.

1 First, I'm sure you're going to like the people here. They're usually friendly and helpful.

2 Remember to bring an umbrella and a raincoat. It often rains a lot in March and April. You should bring some warm clothes, too.

3 Don't forget, you should always say 'please' and 'thank you' when you ask for something. And you shouldn't go to the front of a queue — people hate that here!

I can't wait to see you!

Love,

Jill

b Imagine that your English-speaking penfriend is visiting your country soon. Write a similar letter or email to him/her.

15 How brave!

* First conditional, *when* and *if*
* Vocabulary: adjectives of feeling

1 Read and listen

a How much do you know about gorillas? Mark the statements *T* (true) or *F* (false).

1 Gorillas live in families. ☐

2 Gorillas are dangerous and they often attack people. ☐

3 Gorillas will attack you if you show you're frightened, or if you run away. ☐

b Read the text quickly to check your answers in Exercise 1a.

c What is the text about? Choose one of the topics.

1 A woman who kills a gorilla

2 A woman who takes a baby gorilla back to its family

3 A family of gorillas and how they live

d 🔊 Now read the text again and listen. Answer the questions.

1 Why did the woman take the baby gorilla to the forest?

2 Why didn't the woman run away from the big gorilla?

3 Why did the big gorilla raise his hand?

4 Did the big gorilla take the baby gorilla?

e Find words in the text with these meanings.

1 the opposite of *ill* (paragraph 1) ....

2 know someone because you saw them before (paragraph 1) ....

3 moved up (paragraph 4) ....

f Do you think the woman in the text was brave? Why / Why not?

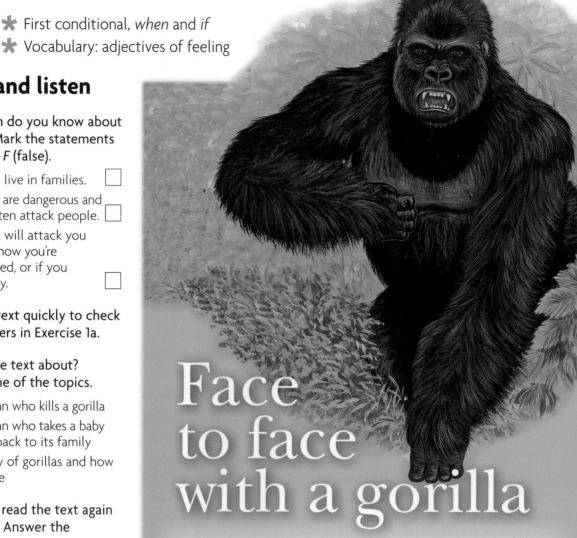

Face to face with a gorilla

I had found the baby gorilla four weeks before, and it was very ill. But now it was well again, and I had to take it back to its family. I picked it up, walked out to the car and drove to the forest. With the baby in my arms, I started to walk in among the trees. I was worried. 'If the mother doesn't recognise the baby, she won't take it back,' I thought. 'Perhaps she'll even kill it.'

The family was there. I put the baby gorilla down on the ground and walked a few metres away. Then I stopped and watched. I could see the mother looking at the baby, and I thought, 'Will she come closer? What will she do?'

Suddenly the father was there, in front of me. He was the biggest gorilla of the family. It was frightening because he was only a metre away. I was frightened, but I knew what to do. People think gorillas often attack people, but they don't – they only attack when you show you're scared. 'If I turn and run away, this gorilla will attack me,' I thought. 'But if I don't move, he'll go away.' I didn't move.

Suddenly the male gorilla lifted his hand. I was terrified. But he wanted to frighten me, not hit me. After a few seconds, he dropped his hand and turned. He went over to the baby, picked it up and moved away into the trees. I sat down on the ground. I was shaking.

2 Grammar

First conditional

(a) Match the two halves of the sentences. Check by looking back at the text on page 118.

1 If I turn and run away,
2 If the mother doesn't recognise the baby,
3 If I don't move,

a he'll go away.
b this gorilla will attack me.
c she won't take it back.

> **Rule:** We use the first conditional to talk about things we think are possible in the future.

(b) Complete the table.

If clause	Result clause	
If + present simple,	.... (will) .... (will not)	+ base form

(c) Put the words into the correct order to make the sentences.

1 see Jane / if / tell / I / I'll / her
   ....

2 my parents / I'm / will / if / late / be angry
   ....

3 I / bring it / I'll / to school tomorrow / if / remember
   ....

4 you'll / new friend, Jake / come / if / you / meet / my / to the party
   ....

5 rain tomorrow / if / the / it / doesn't / we'll / to / beach / go
   ....

6 the concert / if / tonight / I / don't / I / won't / feel better / go / to
   ....

(d) Complete the first conditional sentences with the correct form of the verbs.

1 If Kate ...*gives*... (give) me some help, I .... (finish) my homework in an hour.
2 You ....(not meet) anyone if you .... (not go out).
3 I .... (come) to your party if my mum .... (say) I can.
4 If Ken .... (not want) his ice cream, I .... (eat) it.
5 Susan .... (be) angry if she .... (hear) about this.
6 If we .... (buy) hamburgers, we .... (not have) enough money for the film.

3 Speak

Work with a partner.
Student A: Look at the questions below.
Student B: Turn to page 137.
Ask your questions and answer your partner's.

Student A

1 What will you do if it rains this weekend?
2 What will you do if the weather's nice?
3 How will you feel if your teacher gives you a lot of homework today?
4 What will you wear if you go out this evening?
5 What film will you see if you go to the cinema this week?
6 What programme will you watch if you watch TV this evening?

4 Pronunciation

Stress in conditional sentences

(a) ◁)) Listen to the sentences. Which words are stressed? Why, do you think? <u>Underline</u> the stressed words or syllables.

1 If it <u>rains</u>, I <u>won't go</u> to the <u>beach</u>.
2 We won't pass the test if we don't work hard.
3 I'll give him the card if I see him.
4 If you decide to come, I'll meet you at the cinema.
5 She won't arrive on time if she misses the train.
6 If he doesn't phone his parents, they'll worry about him.

(b) ◁)) Listen again and repeat.

5 Grammar

when and *if*

(a) What is the difference between sentences 1 and 2? Which speaker is sure he will see John?

1 *I'll give John your message when I see him.*

2 *I'll give John your message if I see him.*

(b) Complete the sentences with *if* or *when*.

1 I'm seeing Marta tomorrow. I'll ask her about the book .... I meet her.

2 A: What are you doing tomorrow?
   B: .... there's a good film on, I'll probably go to the cinema.

3 I'm not sure if I want to go to the disco tonight. But .... I decide to go, I'll phone you.

4 It's too hot out in the sun now. Let's play tennis in the evening, ... it's cooler.

6 Vocabulary

Adjectives of feeling

(a) Look at the examples from the text on page 118. Which adjective describes how the woman felt? Which adjective describes the situation?

*It was **frightening** because he was only a metre away.*
*I was **frightened**, but I knew what to do.*

(b) <u>Underline</u> other examples of *-ed* adjectives in the text on page 118.

(c) ◁») Write the adjectives under the pictures. Then listen, check and repeat.

> tired   bored   excited   interested   annoyed   frightened

1 .... 2 .... 3 ....

4 .... 5 .... 6 ....

(d) Circle the correct adjective in each sentence.

1 I didn't like the film. I thought it was *boring* / *bored*.

2 I'm not at all *interesting* / *interested* in history. I prefer thinking about the future.

3 My friend, Elena, is really *frightening* / *frightened* of spiders. She can't stand them!

4 The football match was really *exciting* / *excited*. In the end Manchester United won 3–2.

5 The lesson wasn't very *interesting* / *interested*, so some of the students nearly fell asleep.

6 When I was younger I didn't like watching horror films. I found them too *frightening* / *frightened*.

7 My teacher was very *annoying* / *annoyed* when I told him I didn't have my homework.

8 I found the marathon really *tiring* / *tired* – I slept for 12 hours the next day!

7 Listen and speak

a Look at the pictures. Use a word from each box to label the people.

underwater ~~mountain~~
racing   parachute   fire

driver   fighter   jumper
photographer   ~~climber~~

1 _mountain climber_

2 ....

3 ....

4 ....

5 ....

b Which words can go with each picture? Write the words in the lists.

Nouns:
building   parachute   race   ~~rope~~   shark

Verbs: attack   burn   ~~climb~~   collapse crash   ~~fall~~   land   open   overturn   swim

Picture 1	_rope_	_climb_	_fall_
Picture 2			
Picture 3			
Picture 4			
Picture 5			

c How brave do you think the people are? For each picture, write a score of 1–5 (1 = not very brave, 5 = extremely brave).

Picture 1 ....   Picture 2 ....
Picture 3 ....   Picture 4 ....
Picture 5 ....

d 🔊 Listen to Franco and Jenny. Which three pictures are they talking about? Complete the first column of the table.

	Franco	Jenny
Picture _5_	_2_	....
Picture	....	....
Picture	....	....

e 🔊 Listen again. Write the scores that Franco and Jenny give to each person.

f Work with a partner. Talk about the scores you gave in Exercise 7c.

A: *What score did you give to the mountain climber? I gave her five. I think she's extremely brave.*

B: *I don't think so. I gave her two points because ...*

Dave's risk

8 Read and listen

a 🔊 Look at the title and the photos. What do you think 'Dave's risk' is? Read and listen to find the answer.

Alex: You like Amy a lot, don't you?
Dave: Well, yeah, I do. She's lovely.
Alex: Does she like you too?
Dave: How should I know?
Alex: Ask her out, Dave. Then you'll know.

Maybe I *should* ask Amy to go out with me. But if she doesn't like me, she'll say no. Maybe she'll get angry. Then she won't want to be my friend any more!

Alex: So – did you ask her out?
Dave: No way!
Alex: Come on, Dave. She's a girl, not a monster.
Dave: Ha, ha.
Alex: Look, if you don't try, you'll never know, will you?

Dave: Um, Amy, I was thinking, maybe …
Would you like to go to the cinema tonight?
Amy: Oh, Dave. Sorry, no.
Dave: OK. No big deal. I'm sorry I asked.

Amy: No, Dave, hang on. It's just that today's my father's birthday. But I'd love to go tomorrow.
Dave: Really? Great! There's this old Mel Gibson film on, *Braveheart*. What about that?

b Mark the statements *T* (true) or *F* (false).

1 Dave likes Amy.
2 Dave isn't sure how much Amy likes him.
3 Alex isn't interested in Dave's problem.

4 Dave doesn't want to lose Amy as a friend.
5 Amy says she doesn't want to go to the cinema with Dave.
6 Amy's dad doesn't want her to go out with Dave.

9 Everyday English

(a) Find expressions 1–4 in the photo story. Who says them? Match them with expressions a–d.

1	How should I know?	a	Wait.
2	No way!	b	No!
3	Hang on.	c	It isn't important.
4	No big deal.	d	I have no idea.

(b) How do you say expressions 1–4 in your language?

(c) Read the dialogues. Fill in the spaces with expressions 1–4 in Exercise 9a.

1 **Julie:** Come on, Mike. We have to leave now.
   Mike: _____ a minute. I'm just going to get my jacket.

2 **Paolo:** What time does the football match begin?
   Martina: _____ Why don't you ask Mario?

3 **Tony:** Can you lend me a pound?
   Simon: _____ You won't give it back, I know.

4 **Judith:** Sorry, I can't help you right now.
   Alice: _____ I'll do it myself.

10 Write

(a) Read what Geraldine wrote about a book she read. Answer the questions.

1 What was the book/film/programme?
2 Who was the main character?
3 Where was he/she?
4 Why was he/she in danger?
5 What did he/she do?
6 How did the story end?

The book I read is 'A Picture to Remember' by Sarah Scott-Malden. It's about a girl called Christina. One day, she saw two men in a car. One of them had a gun. They were bank robbers and she saw their faces. They didn't want her to tell the police, so they planned to kill her.

First, one of the robbers attacked her at the gym, but luckily she only hurt her arm. After this, she was in the street with her friend, Philippe, when one of the robbers drove his car into them. Philippe was hurt and had to go to hospital.

Christina went to visit Philippe. When she left the hospital in her car, the robbers followed her. Christina saw that they had a gun and understood that they wanted to kill her. She was frightened, but she kept calm. The robbers were close behind her, but they were driving too fast and couldn't stop. They crashed their car and it overturned. One of the robbers died and the police caught the other one.

(b) Write about a film, book or TV programme where somebody was in a dangerous situation. Use the questions and Geraldine's text to help you.

For your portfolio

It's a mad world

* Present perfect + *ever/never*
* Vocabulary: verb and noun pairs

1 Read and listen

(a) Read the texts quickly and match the paragraphs with the pictures.

Have you ever seen anything like it?

People have done some strange things to get into the record books! Here are some of them.

1 Len Vale Onslow is 103 years old. He's the oldest man in Britain with a licence to ride a motorbike, and he's never had an accident!

2 Hu Saelao, from Thailand, holds the world record for the longest human hair. His hair is 5.15 metres long – he's never cut it.

3 Strong man John Evans balances things on his head for ten seconds each time. At different times, John has balanced 62 books, 101 bricks, 548 footballs, even a Mini car!

4 Susan Smith, from Philadelphia, is probably the laziest woman on earth! The last time she got out of bed was 27 years ago.

5 Mel Ednie lives in Scotland, and he grows onions – big onions! He has broken the world record three times. In 1995, Mel grew an onion that weighed 7.2kg.

(b) 🔊 Now read the text again and listen. One of the texts is not true. Which one, do you think? (The answer is on page 129.)

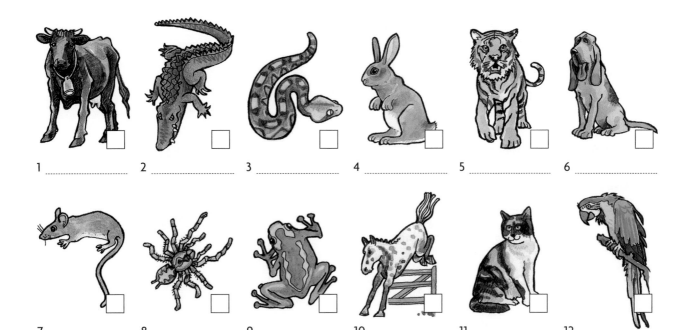

1 .... 2 .... 3 .... 4 .... 5 .... 6 ....

7 .... 8 .... 9 .... 10 .... 11 .... 12 ....

2 Vocabulary

Animals

🔊 Write the names of the animals in the pictures. Then listen, check and repeat.

> frog   horse   tiger
> rabbit   cow   parrot
> dog   alligator   mouse
> tarantula   cat   snake

3 Listen

a 🔊 Mr Brown wants to become a world record-holder. What record does he want? Listen to the first part of an interview with him to check your ideas.

Mr George Brown

b 🔊 Listen again and look at the pictures in Exercise 2. Tick the animals that Mr Brown has in his house.

c 🔊 Check that you understand the words in the box. Then listen to the second part of the interview and fill in the missing words.

> record   never   frogs   dangerous   woman   parrot   room

Interviewer: Is it difficult to have so many animals all in the same house?

Mr Brown: Sometimes. You see, I can't have the alligator in the same ^{1} .... as the other animals. It's eaten some of the smaller ones. It loves ^{2} ....

Interviewer: Yes, I see. So have you ever had any problems yourself? Some of these animals are ^{3} .... , aren't they?

Mr Brown: Well, the tarantulas have bitten me once or twice.

Interviewer: What do your neighbours think about all these animals?

Mr Brown: Well, they've ^{4} .... complained.

Interviewer: Have any of your pets ever escaped?

Mr Brown: Yes. The ^{5} .... escaped in 1998. But the alligator and the tarantulas have never escaped.

Interviewer: Oh, good! And tell me, Mr Brown, how many animals do you need to break the ^{6} .... ?

Mr Brown: Well, unfortunately, there's a ^{7} .... in America with more than 60 pets in her house, so I have a long way to go.

d Match the two parts of each sentence.

1	Mr Brown	a	have never complained about the pets.
2	The tarantulas	b	has escaped once.
3	The alligator	c	has had some problems with his pets.
4	His neighbours	d	has eaten several small pets in the house.
5	The parrot	e	have bitten him.

e Do you think Mr Brown is crazy? Why / Why not?

4 Grammar

Present perfect + *ever/never*

a Look at the examples.
Complete the rule and the table.

*People **have done** some strange things.*
*John **has balanced** a Mini car on his head.*
*He's never **cut** his hair.*
***Have** you ever **seen** anything like it?*

Rule: We use the present perfect to talk about actions that happened some time up to now.

We form the present perfect with the present tense of .... + past participle.

Positive	Negative	Questions	Short answers
I/you/we/they 've (............) worked	I/you/we/they **haven't** (have not) worked	.... I/you/we/they worked?	Yes, I/you/we/they **have**. No, I/you/we/they **haven't**.
he/she/it 's (............) work**ed**	he/she/it 's (............) work**ed**	.... he/she/it work**ed**?	Yes, he/she/it **has**. No, he/she/it **hasn't**.

b Fill in the verb forms.
Use the Irregular verbs list on page 138 to help you.

Base form	Past participle
1 be	*been*
2 do	....
3 go	....
4 see	....
5 write	....
6 bite	....
7 speak	....
8 eat	....
9 drive	....
10 fly	....
11 swim	....
12 win	....

c Complete the sentences. Use the present perfect form of the verbs.

1 We *'ve never lived* (never/live) in a foreign country.
2 .... she .... (ever/study) a foreign language?
3 I .... (never/see) a tarantula.
4 .... you .... (ever/drive) a car?
5 .... they .... (ever/fly) in a helicopter?
6 Jack .... (stay) in Japan, but he .... (never/eat) sushi.

5 Pronunciation

***have* and *has* in the present perfect**

a 🔊 Listen to the questions and answers.
How are *have* and *has* pronounced? Listen again and repeat.

A: *Have you ever driven a car?*
B: *Yes, I have.*
A: *Has she ever studied a foreign language?*
B: *Yes, she has.*

b 🔊 Underline the stressed syllables. Then listen and repeat.

1 I've never lived in America.
2 Have you ever seen an alligator? No, I haven't.
3 Has he ever swum in a river? Yes, he has.

6 Speak

a Work with a partner. Ask and answer the questions.

1 ever / see / a tiger?
2 ever / eat / Chinese food?
3 ever / be / on TV?
4 ever / speak / to a British person?
5 ever / win / any money?

A: *Have you ever seen a tiger?*
B: *No, never. Have you ever eaten Chinese food?*
A: *Yes, I have.*

b Work with a partner or in a small group. Ask and answer about things you have done in your life. Use some of the verbs in the box.

travel	stay	play	win
eat	fly	drive	meet

7 Read

a) Look at the picture of John Evans on page 124. Then look at the pictures on this page. Which of these things do you think John balances on his head? Read the text and check your ideas.

John Evans, the Headbalancer

John Evans has been in *The Guinness Book of Records* 29 times! Each time, it was for balancing things on his head. He has balanced some amazing things on his head: bricks, cans of cola, books, footballs – even a car, and two girls on bicycles!

John was a builder and he often carried bricks on his head when he was building houses. He usually carried around 24 or 25, but in 1997 he stood with 101 bricks on his head.

John first broke a record in 1992, when he balanced 84 milk crates. Now he has broken that record too. In 2001 he balanced 96 milk crates, all on his head! He has been on TV in Britain many times, and in 1998 he was on American TV twice.

When John started breaking records and appearing on TV shows, he decided to raise money for charity. So far, he has raised over £56,000.

b) Now read the text again and answer the questions.

1. How many times has John Evans been in *The Guinness Book of Records*?
2. What did John do before he became a record-breaker?
3. How did he start to balance things on his head?
4. When did he first break a record?
5. What happened in 2001?
6. When did John decide to start raising money for charity?
7. Does John still raise money for charity? How much money has he raised?

c) Do you know anyone who has done things for charity? If yes, what has he/she done? Have you ever done something for charity?

8 Vocabulary
Verb and noun pairs

a) Look at the examples of verb and noun pairs from the text in Exercise 7.

*John first **broke a record** in 1992.*
*He decided to **raise money** for charity.*

Match the verbs with the nouns.

Verbs		Nouns	
1	raise	a	a risk
2	win	b	a prize
3	break	c	a joke
4	build	d	a record
5	tell	e	money
6	take	f	a house

b) Complete the sentences. Use the correct verb.

1. In the 1968 Olympics long jump, Bob Beamon _____ the gold medal, and he _____ the world record.
2. At the moment, Sandro's parents are _____ a new house.
3. The charity Oxfam _____ lots of money every year for poor people.
4. Esra _____ a risk when she rode her bike without a helmet.
5. I like Steve because he _____ really good jokes.

9 Read

(a) Look at the photos. Who is the singer in the bottom left photo? What do you know about him? Who are the other people? Read the text and check your ideas.

(b) Now read the text again. Match the numbers and places with the information.

1	25	a	the name of Elvis's house
2	1977	b	the number of albums he has sold
3	Graceland	c	the place which holds the biggest look-alike competition
4	1956	d	in 2002, the number of years after Elvis's death
5	1,000,000,000	e	the year he died
6	Memphis	f	the year of his first hit record

ELVIS LIVES!

Elvis Presley recorded his first song in 1954 and had his first hit in 1956 with *Heartbreak Hotel*. After that, Elvis produced one hit after another and became 'the King' for millions of fans. Today he remains the world's most successful singer, with a sales record of over a billion albums.

In 1977 at Graceland, his home in Memphis, Tennessee, Elvis died.

Or did he? Through the years, fans have kept seeing him. Lots of people say they have seen his ghost at Graceland – near the pool, in the garden or looking through a window. But also, there are thousands of people who refuse to believe that he died at all. They have reported 'sightings' of Elvis in every part of the world.

And Elvis is alive in another way. All over the world, there are people who try to sing, dress, move and speak like him.

Elvis 'look-alike' competitions happen all the time – the biggest one, in Memphis, is a huge international event. You'll find Elvises everywhere – they appear in Germany and Sweden and Denmark.

There are Chinese, Taiwanese, Thai and Japanese Elvises. There are middle-aged, teenage and child Elvises, female Elvises, blind Elvises and Elvises in wheelchairs. In Las Vegas you can be married at the Graceland Chapel by a look-alike who sings Elvis songs. A group of sky-divers called the Flying Elvi come down in parachutes to perform as Elvis. And so on.

Some of the most successful look-alikes have their own fan clubs and websites. Some of them stay 'in character' 24 hours a day – it seems they have almost *become* Elvis. A popular joke tells how Elvis himself entered one of the big look-alike competitions ... and came third.

In 2002, the world celebrated the 25th anniversary of Elvis's death. As one fan said, 'It's 25 years later, and he's bigger than ever. People love him, and they just don't want to let go. He's still the King.'

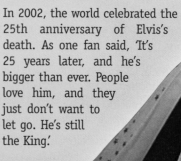

(c) Find words in the text on page 128 with these meanings.

1 successful pop record (paragraph 1) ....
2 people who love a famous person (paragraph 1) ....
3 very large (paragraph 5) ....
4 between 40 and 60 years old (paragraph 6) ....
5 moving chairs for people who can't walk (paragraph 6) ....
6 date when something happened in a past year (paragraph 8) ....

(d) Have you ever seen someone perform as Elvis, or as some other famous person? Why do you think people do this, and why are their performances so popular?

10 Write

(a) Imagine you are staying with an American family in Los Angeles. You have received this letter from a friend. What topics does she ask about?

> Dear .... (your name)
>
> How are you? Are you enjoying yourself in Los Angeles? I hope your journey there was OK, and you weren't too tired when you arrived.
>
> Please tell me all about the family you're staying with. What are they like? What have you done and seen in Los Angeles? Have you met any interesting people? Have you visited Hollywood and have you seen any film stars?
>
> I'm having a good time. I've started horse-riding lessons, so I'm sending a photo of me on Fury, one of the horses at our riding school. I've also finished all my exams (great!) and my sister has passed her driving test, so now she can drive me everywhere!
>
> Please write soon.
>
> Love,
>
> Louise

(b) Write a letter or an email in reply to Louise. Start like this:

> Dear Louise,
>
> Thanks for your letter and the photo. It was great to hear from you.
>
> I'm having a fantastic time here in Los Angeles.

For your portfolio

page 124, Exercise 1b Text 4 is not true.

Module 4 Check your progress

1 Grammar

a Complete the sentences. Use the verbs in the box with the correct form of *be going to*.

> visit   help   ~~rain~~   dance   wear
> not ride   not watch

1 Look at those clouds. It _'s going to rain_ .
2 I've got a difficult History project to do.
   My sister _____ me with it.
3 I _____ television tonight. All
   the programmes are boring!
4 _____ you _____ your black
   jeans tonight?
5 My parents _____ my
   grandfather at the weekend.
6 Peter doesn't like horses. He _____
   with us this afternoon.
7 There's a party next Friday night,
   and we _____ all night! **6**

b Complete each sentence with *must* or *mustn't*.

1 Come on, Julie! We _mustn't_ be late!
2 It's a great book. You really _____ read it.
3 Sorry, Jimmy, I'm late. I _____ go now.
4 You _____ tell anyone about this! It's too
   embarrassing.
5 Diane, turn the music down! You _____
   play it so loudly!
6 I can go out with you tonight, but I _____
   be home before midnight.
7 OK, you can have a pet snake – but it
   _____ come into the house! **6**

c Complete the sentences with *should* or *shouldn't*.

1 You _shouldn't_ eat a lot of fried food.
2 I _____ take up running. I'd like to be
   fitter.
3 When you wait for a bus in Britain, you
   _____ stand in the queue.
4 They _____ get some exercise. They
   _____ spend so much time in front of
   the computer.
5 You look great! You _____ worry about
   losing weight!
6 Maria is feeling ill. _____ we take
   her to the doctor? **6**

d Complete the first conditional sentences with the correct form of the verbs.

1 If you _help_ (help) me, I _____ (buy)
   you an ice cream.
2 If Jack _____ (come) to school late, the
   teacher _____ (be) really angry.
3 The neighbours _____ (complain) if we
   _____ (make) a lot of noise.
4 If I _____ (have) time, I _____ (get)
   the tickets this afternoon.
5 If you _____ (not get up) now,
   you _____ (not have) any breakfast.
6 Annette _____ (not pass) her test
   if she _____ (not study) harder. **11**

e Write sentences in the present perfect.

1 I / never / see / a tarantula.
   I've never seen a tarantula.
2 My brother / never / study / a foreign
   language.
   _____
3 My parents / never / fly / in a plane.
   _____
4 I / never / get / 100% in a test.
   _____
5 Richard / never / eat / frogs' legs.
   _____
6 your teacher / ever / shout / at you?
   _____ ?
7 you / ever / speak / to a British person?
   _____ ?
8 your parents / ever / win / a competition?
   _____ ? **7**

2 Vocabulary

a Write the opposites of the adjectives.

1 honest   _dishonest_
2 kind   _____
3 organised   _____
4 cheerful   _____
5 friendly   _____
6 polite   _____
7 hard-working _____ **6**

b Complete the adjectives with the *-ed* or *-ing* ending.

1 I was really tir *ed* last night when I went to bed. Yesterday was a very tir_____ day.

2 We were excit_____ about going to the football, but in the end it was a bor_____ match.

3 I thought the Dracula film was quite frighten_____ , but my girlfriend wasn't frighten_____ at all.

4 We went to a museum last Sunday. My parents thought it was fascinat_____ , but I wasn't really interest_____ .

	7

c Find nine more animals in the wordsquare.

R	A	B	A	I	P	A	R	G	O
T	R	V	L	T	A	R	A	N	T
A	G	U	L	S	R	A	X	T	I
R	I	Q	I	L	R	O	D	O	G
F	R	O	G	M	O	U	S	R	E
T	A	R	A	N	T	U	L	A	R
H	A	M	T	E	R	T	I	B	R
O	W	M	O	U	S	E	J	B	A
R	H	O	R	S	E	B	F	I	B
S	N	A	K	E	F	R	O	T	T

	9

d Complete the sentences. Use the correct form of the verbs in the box.

raise	win	break	~~build~~	tell	take

1 My aunt and uncle are _building_ a house in the country at the moment.

2 I've been in a lot of competitions, but I've never _____ a prize.

3 If you want to succeed, you sometimes have to _____ risks.

4 People always laugh when Terry _____ a joke.

5 We're having a 'Fun Week' at school in October. We want to _____ money for sports equipment.

6 Joanna came first in her race and _____ the school record.

	5

3 Everyday English

Complete the dialogues with the words in the box.

It's no big deal	No way	~~I'll pick up~~
How should I know	Hang on	

Carla: Matt, what are you doing next Saturday?

Matt: Saturday?

Carla: Yes. 4Tune are giving a concert, and I think it's going to be really good. If you like, [1] _I'll pick up_ some tickets this afternoon, and then ...

Matt: [2] _____ , Carla! Sorry, but I can't make it. I'm going to my grandparents' next weekend.

Carla: Oh, OK, that's fine. [3] _____ . I'll go with Ben and Lisa.

Matt: Sorry about that.

Carla: Do you like visiting your grandparents?

Matt: Yes, I do. Sunday lunch is the best bit. My granny cooks wonderful fish and chips.

Carla: Oh, Matt! How many calories are there in a plate of fish and chips?

Matt: [4] _____ ? I haven't got any idea.

Carla: Hundreds! If you eat that, you'll get fat.

Matt: No, I'll never get fat!

Carla: Are you sure? I can imagine you when you're 35 – big and fat!

Matt: [5] _____ ! That won't happen to me!

	4

How did you do?

Tick (✓) a box for each section.

Total score	☺ Very good	☺ OK	☹ Not very good
☐ 67			
Grammar	27 – 36	20 – 26	less than 20
Vocabulary	20 – 27	15 – 19	less than 15
Everyday English	3 – 4	2	less than 2

Project 1
A class survey

1 Prepare the survey

(a) Work in a small group (three or four students). Choose one of the following topics:

- Hobbies and interests
- Housework
- Eating habits

(b) In your group, think of five questions that you can ask other students about your topic, for example:

Eating habits

How often do you eat take-away food?

Do you eat a big breakfast every day?

How many times a week do you eat fresh fruit?

(c) Make a questionnaire with your questions, like this:

> 1 How often do you eat take-away food?
>   never ☐
>   once or twice a month ☐
>   once a week ☐
>   more than once a week ☐
>
> 2 Do you eat a big breakfast every day?
>   yes ☐
>   no ☐

Make sure that everyone in your group has a copy of the questionnaire.

(d) Use your questionnaire. Ask as many other students in your class as you can, and make a note of their answers.

2 Write up the results

(a) Go back to your group and put all your answers together. For some questions, you can draw a chart.

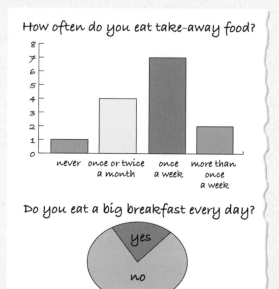

How often do you eat take-away food?

Do you eat a big breakfast every day?

(b) Write sentences about your answers, for example:

> Only one student in our class never eats take-away food. Four students eat take-away food once or twice a month, and half the class eat it once a week.

(c) Arrange your sentences and charts on poster paper, under your topic heading. Add illustrations if you want to.

3 Present your information

Use your poster to make a group presentation to the rest of the class.

Project 2

A presentation on a successful person

1 Brainstorm

(a) Look through Module 2 to find texts that give information about successful and creative people. Quickly read through these texts again.

(b) Think of a successful person you want to find out about. The person might be:

- an inventor
- an artist or writer
- a politician
- a film director
- a musician
- something else

(c) Work in a group and appoint one student to take notes. Brainstorm ideas to decide which person you will do your project on. What do you know about this person, and what do you want to find out?

2 Research

With a partner or on your own, find out as much as possible about the person you are working on. Use the Internet or look up information in books or magazines, in a library or at home.

Questions to think about:

- When was he/she born?
- What can you find out about his/her childhood?
- What did he/she do/invent/create?
- What was his/her biggest success?
- Why was/is this person so successful?

3 Presentation

In your group, put together all the information you have. Decide how you will organise your presentation. For example:

- Start with a picture or a piece of music. Ask the class to guess who your presentation is going to be about.

- Take it in turns to present the facts about the person.

- Finish your presentation with each member of the group saying what they admire most about the person.

For your portfolio

Project 3

A poster about the future

1 Brainstorm

a You are going to make a poster and give a presentation about life in the future. Work in a group of four or five. In your group, decide on a topic that you all want to work on. For example:

- homes
- towns and cities
- transport
- schools
- clothes
- food
- communication
- weather
- something else

b In your group, decide how far into the future you want to look. Will you talk about the year 2025? 2100? 3000 ...?

c Think about what life will be like in the year you chose. For example, if you chose the topic *Food*, you can think about these questions:

- Will people eat healthy food?
- Where will their food come from?
- Will they eat more take-away meals?
- Do you think the food will be good to eat?
- Will it be more expensive?
- Will there be enough food for everybody?

Brainstorm ideas and make notes.

2 Make the poster

a Find or draw some pictures that fit with your ideas on the topic. For example, you can find photos from science fiction films in magazines or on the Internet, or you can draw your own pictures.

b Write short texts for each of the pictures you are going to use. For example:

> In the year 2050, robots will do the housework in most people's homes.

c At the top of your project paper, write the title of your presentation. For example:

> HOMES IN THE YEAR 2050

Arrange your pictures and short texts on the paper, but leave space at the bottom.

d At the bottom of the poster, write a longer text together. Say what you think about the future you are predicting. For example:

> Homes will be small, but they will be clean and comfortable. People will enjoy living at home because they won't have to do any housework.

3 Presentation

Present your poster to the other students in your class. Be ready to answer questions about it.

For your portfolio

Project 4

A talk on an event that happened this year

1 Listen

🔊 Listen to the beginning of three talks about memorable events that happened this year. What were the events?

2 Choose a topic

Spend some time thinking about the event that you will choose. Will you talk about an event that happened to you or an event that happened somewhere else in the world? Will you talk about something sad, something happy or something funny?

3 Plan

(a) Think about these questions:

- When and where did the event take place?
- Is there any background information that you will need to explain the event?
- What happened, exactly?
- Why was it memorable? How did you feel about it at the time? How do you feel about it now?

(b) Make a list of important words you will want to use. If you aren't sure of some words, look them up in a dictionary or ask your teacher. Then use the words to help you make notes for your talk. Don't write everything down in complete sentences – just write important phrases that will help you to remember what you want to say.

(c) Collect any information you need about your topic. If you can, collect pictures, drawings or photographs that might help you to make your talk more interesting.

(d) Practise your talk quietly to yourself.

4 Give the talk

Work in a group of four or five. Each student gives his/her talk to the others in the group. Be prepared to answer questions at the end of your talk.

For your portfolio

✳ Speaking exercises: extra material

Starter section, page 13, Exercise 3b

Student B: Look at the information about Wendford.

Ask your partner about these things in Langton.

cafés   station   discos   library   sports stadium

swimming pools   airport

B: *Are there any cafés?*
A: *Yes, there are _____ cafés.*
    No, there aren't.

B: *Is there a station?*
A: *Yes, there is.*
    No, there isn't.

Wendford info

- library
- sports stadium
- 2 discos
- station
- no swimming pool
- 5 cafés
- no airport

Unit 8, page 69, Exercise 3

Student B: Look at the picture of Nick's desk. Find out what is different in your partner's picture. Take it in turns to ask and answer.

B: *Is/Are there any ... in your picture?*
A: *Yes, there's / there are some ...*   *No, there isn't/aren't any ...*

Unit 14, page 113, Exercise 3

Student B: Read the role card.
Take it in turns to listen to your partner's problem and give advice with *should* or *shouldn't*.

Student B

You love football and you love your favourite football team. But you have a problem. You are going to your best friend's birthday party on Saturday. But now you know that your team has an important match on Saturday, too. You want to see the match but you don't want to hurt your friend. Should you go to the match? Should you go to the party? Ask Student A.

Unit 15, page 119, Exercise 3

Student B: Look at the questions. Ask your questions and answer you partner's.

Student B

1 What will you do if you stay at home this weekend?
2 What will you study if you go to university?
3 What will you buy if you go shopping this weekend?
4 How will you feel if your parents ask you to do a lot of housework this evening?
5 Where will you travel if you go abroad on holiday this year?
6 Where will you go if you meet your friends tonight?

* Irregular verbs and phonetics

Irregular verbs

Base form	Past simple	Past participle
be	was/were	been
beat	beat	beaten
become	became	become
begin	began	begun
bite	bit	bitten
break	broke	broken
build	built	built
buy	bought	bought
can	could	could
catch	caught	caught
choose	chose	chosen
come	came	come
cut	cut	cut
do	did	done
drive	drove	driven
eat	ate	eaten
fall	fell	fallen
feel	felt	felt
find	found	found
fly	flew	flown
get	got	got
give	gave	given
go	went	gone
grow	grew	grown
have	had	had
hear	heard	heard
hit	hit	hit
hurt	hurt	hurt
keep	kept	kept
know	knew	known
leave	left	left
lose	lost	lost
make	made	made
meet	met	met
put	put	put
read	read	read
ride	rode	ridden
run	ran	run
say	said	said
see	saw	seen
sell	sold	sold
send	sent	sent
sit	sat	sat
sleep	slept	slept
speak	spoke	spoken
stand	stood	stood
swim	swam	swum
take	took	taken
teach	taught	taught
tell	told	told
think	thought	thought
throw	threw	thrown
understand	understood	understood
wake	woke	woke
win	won	won
write	wrote	written

Phonetic symbols

Consonants

/p/	pen
/b/	be
/t/	two
/d/	do
/k/	can
/g/	good
/f/	five
/v/	very
/m/	make
/n/	nice
/ŋ/	sing
/s/	see
/z/	trousers
/w/	we
/l/	listen
/r/	right
/j/	you
/h/	he
/θ/	thing
/ð/	this
/ʃ/	she
/tʃ/	cheese
/ʒ/	usually
/dʒ/	German

Vowels

/æ/	man
/ɑː/	father
/e/	ten
/ɜː/	thirteen
/ə/	mother
/ɪ/	sit
/iː/	see
/ʊ/	book
/uː/	food
/ʌ/	up
/ɒ/	hot
/ɔː/	four

Diphthongs

/eɪ/	great
/aɪ/	fine
/ɔɪ/	boy
/ɪə/	hear
/eə/	chair
/aʊ/	town
/əʊ/	go
/ʊə/	pure

Wordlist

(v) = verb   (n) = noun   (adj) = adjective

Starter Unit

Countries and nationalities

America /əˈmerɪkə/
American /əˈmerɪkən/
Argentina /ˌɑːdʒənˈtiːnə/
Argentinian
    /ˌɑːdʒənˈtɪniən/
Belgian /ˈbeldʒən/
Belgium /ˈbeldʒəm/
Brazil /brəˈzɪl/
Brazilian /brəˈzɪliən/
Britain /ˈbrɪtən/
British /ˈbrɪtɪʃ/
Canada /ˈkænədə/
Canadian /kəˈneɪdiən/
China /ˈtʃaɪnə/
Chinese /tʃaɪˈniːz/
France /frɑːns/
French /frenʃ/
German /ˈdʒɜːmən/
Germany /ˈdʒɜːməni/
Italian /ɪˈtæliən/
Italy /ˈɪtəli/
Japan /dʒəˈpæn/
Japanese /ˌdʒæpəˈniːz/
Poland /ˈpəʊlənd/
Polish /ˈpəʊlɪʃ/
Russia /ˈrʌʃə/
Russian /ˈrʌʃən/
Spain /speɪn/
Spanish /ˈspænɪʃ/
Swiss /swɪs/
Switzerland /ˈswɪtsələnd/
USA /ˌjuːesˈeɪ/

Family

aunt /ɑːnt/
brother /ˈbrʌðər/
child /tʃaɪld/
children /ˈtʃɪldrən/
father /ˈfɑːðər/
grandfather /ˈgrænˌfɑːðər/
grandmother
    /ˈgrænˌmʌðər/
mother /ˈmʌðər/
parent /ˈpeərənt/
sister /ˈsɪstər/
uncle /ˈʌŋkl/

Food

apple /ˈæpl/
banana /bəˈnɑːnə/
dish /dɪʃ/

ice cream /ˌaɪsˈkriːm/
orange /ˈɒrɪndʒ/
pizza /ˈpiːtsə/

Clothes

dress /dres/
jacket /ˈdʒækɪt/
jeans /dʒiːnz/
jumper /ˈdʒʌmpər/
scarf /skɑːf/
shirt /ʃɜːt/
shoe /ʃuː/
skirt /skɜːt/
socks /sɒks/

House/furniture

armchair /ˈɑːmtʃeər/
bath /bɑːθ/
bed /bed/
chair /tʃeər/
cooker /ˈkʊkər/
cupboard /ˈkʌbəd/
fridge /frɪdʒ/
picture /ˈpɪktʃər/
shower /ˈʃaʊər/
sink /sɪŋk/
sofa /ˈsəʊfə/
table /ˈteɪbl/
telephone /ˈtelɪfəʊn/
toilet /ˈtɔɪlɪt/
window /ˈwɪndəʊ/

School/college

book /bʊk/
friend /frend/
lesson /ˈlesən/
letter /ˈletər/
library /ˈlaɪbrəri/
ruler /ˈruːlər/
science /saɪəns/
student /ˈstjuːdənt/
test /test/
university /ˌjuːnɪˈvɜːsəti/

Town

airport /ˈeəpɔːt/
bookshop /ˈbʊkʃɒp/
bicycle /ˈbaɪsɪkl/
café /ˈkæfeɪ/
car /kɑːr/
cinema /ˈsɪnəmə/
clothes shop /kləʊðz ʃɒp/
disco /ˈdɪskəʊ/
film /fɪlm/
flat /flæt/

house /haʊs/
language school
    /ˈlæŋgwɪdʒ skuːl/
museum /mjuːˈziːəm/
music shop /ˈmjuːzɪk ʃɒp/
park /pɑːk/
policeman /pəˈliːsmən/
post office /ˈpəʊst ˌɒfɪs/
river /ˈrɪvər/
shoe shop /ʃuː ʃɒp/
shop /ʃɒp/
sports stadium
    /ˈspɔːts ˌsteɪdiəm/
station /ˈsteɪʃən/
street /striːt/
supermarket
    /ˈsuːpəˌmɑːkɪt/
swimming pool
    /ˈswɪmɪŋ puːl/
train /treɪn/

Time and dates

spring /sprɪŋ/
summer /ˈsʌmər/
autumn /ˈɔːtəm/
winter /ˈwɪntər/

Monday /ˈmʌndeɪ/
Tuesday /ˈtjuːzdeɪ/
Wednesday /ˈwenzdeɪ/
Thursday /ˈθɜːzdeɪ/
Friday /ˈfraɪdeɪ/
Saturday /ˈsætədeɪ/
Sunday /ˈsʌndeɪ/

January /ˈdʒænjuəri/
February /ˈfebruəri/
March /mɑːtʃ/
April /ˈeɪprəl/
May /meɪ/
June /dʒuːn/
July /dʒʊˈlaɪ/
August /ˈɔːgəst/
September /sepˈtembər/
October /ɒkˈtəʊbər/
November /nəˈvembər/
December /dɪˈsembər/

birthday /ˈbɜːθdeɪ/
day /deɪ/
month /mʌnθ/
today /təˈdeɪ/
tomorrow /təˈmɒrəʊ/
week /wiːk/

Verbs

close /kləʊz/
cry /kraɪ/
have got /hæv gɒt/
jump /dʒʌmp/
know /nəʊ/
laugh /lɑːf/
listen /ˈlɪsən/
look at /lʊk æt/
open /ˈəʊpən/
paint /peɪnt/
play /pleɪ/
prefer /prɪˈfɜːr/
read /riːd/
run /rʌn/
shout /ʃaʊt/
smile /smaɪl/
swim /swɪm/
take a photo /teɪk ə
    ˈfəʊtəʊ/
tell /tel/

Adjectives

big /bɪg/
dangerous /ˈdeɪndʒərəs/
expensive /ɪkˈspensɪv/
fair (hair) /feər/
favourite /ˈfeɪvərɪt/
fine /faɪn/
funny /ˈfʌni/
heavy /ˈhevi/
interesting /ˈɪntrəstɪŋ/
lovely /ˈlʌvli/
new /njuː/
small /smɔːl/

Prepositions

behind /bɪˈhaɪnd/
between /bɪˈtwiːn/
in /ɪn/
near /nɪər/
next to /nekst tuː/
on /ɒn/
under /ˈʌndər/

Phrases

I'd like ... /aɪd laɪk/
I'm fine, thanks.
    /aɪm faɪn θæŋks/
My name's ... /maɪ neɪmz/
Nice to meet you.
    /naɪs tə miːt juː/
Thank you very much.
    /θæŋk juː ˈveri mʌtʃ/

Unit 1

Hobbies and interests

ballet (n) /'bæleɪ/
computer (n) /kəm'pju:tər/
Formula 1 (n) /'fɔ:mjələ wʌn/
guitar (n) /gɪ'tɑːr/
helicopter (n) /'helɪkɒptər/
pilot (n) /'paɪlət/
pop music (n) /'pɒp ,mju:zɪk/
race (n) /reɪs/
sport (n) /spɔːt/
swimming (n) /'swɪmɪŋ/
tennis (n) /'tenɪs/

Verbs

care /keər/
dance /dɑːns/
drive /draɪv/
enjoy /ɪn'dʒɔɪ/
fly /flaɪ/
get up /get 'ʌp/
hate /heɪt/
land /lænd/
learn /lɜːn/
like /laɪk/
listen to /'lɪsən tuː/
look down at /lʊk 'daʊn ət/
play (computer games) /pleɪ
ride /raɪd/
sleep /sliːp/
start /stɑːt/
stop /stɒp/
study /'stʌdi/
take off /teɪk 'ɒf/
talk to /'tɔːk tuː/
teach /tiːtʃ/
want /wɒnt/
watch /wɒtʃ/

Everyday English

guy /gaɪ/
Shut up! /ʃʌt 'ʌp/
So what? /səʊ 'wɒt/
That's weird! /ðæts 'wɪəd/
What about him/her? /wɒt ə,baʊt 'hɪm/

Unit 2

School

Advanced Maths (n) /əd'vɑːnst mæθs/
Art (n) /ɑːt/
assembly (n) /ə'sembli/
athletics (n) /æθ'letɪks/
Biology (n) /baɪ'ɒlədʒi/
break (n) /breɪk/
Drama (n) /'drɑːmə/
exam (n) /ɪg'zæm/
free time (n) /friː 'taɪm/
French (n) /frentʃ/
Geography (n) /dʒi'ɒgrəfi/
headteacher (n) /hed'tiːtʃə/
History (n) /'hɪstəri/
homework (n) /'həʊmwɜːk/
Information Technology (IT) (n) /,ɪnfə'meɪʃən tek'nɒlədʒi/
Maths (n) /mæθs/
photography (n) /fə'tɒgrəfi/
Physical Education (PE) (n) /,fɪzɪkəl edʒʊ'keɪʃən/
Physics (n) /'fɪzɪks/
school hall (n) /skuːl 'hɔːl/
sports club (n) /'spɔːts klʌb/
subject (n) /'sʌbdʒɪkt/
tie (n) /taɪ/
timetable (n) /'taɪm,teɪbl/
uniform (n) /'juːnɪfɔːm/

Frequency expressions

always /'ɔːlweɪz/
hardly ever /hɑːdlɪ 'evər/
never /'nevər/
often /'ɒfən/
once (a week/month/year) /wʌns/
sometimes /'sʌmtaɪmz/
three times (a week) /θriː taɪmz/
twice (a week) /twaɪs/
usually /'juːʒəli/

Verbs

belong to /bɪ'lɒŋ tuː/
choose /tʃuːz/
cook /kʊk/
eat /iːt/
find /faɪnd/
finish /'fɪnɪʃ/
get dressed /get 'drest/
go swimming /gəʊ 'swɪmɪŋ/
go to bed /gəʊ tə 'bed/
help /help/
rain /reɪn/
see /siː/
spend (time) /spend/
stay /steɪ/
walk /wɔːk/
wear /weər/

Adjectives

late /leɪt/
lonely /'ləʊnli/
quiet /kwaɪət/
similar /'sɪmɪlər/

Unit 3

Housework

clean (v) /kliːn/
cook (v) / do the cooking (v) /kʊk/, /duː ðə kʊkɪŋ/
housework (n) /'haʊswɜːk/
ironing (n) /'aɪənɪŋ/
shopping (n) /'ʃɒpɪŋ/
washing (n) /'wɒʃɪŋ/
washing-up (n) /,wɒʃɪŋ'ʌp/

Time expressions

at the moment /ət ðə 'məʊmənt/
every (day/evening/ weekend) /'evri/
next (year) /nekst/
now/right now /raɪt naʊ/
this (morning/afternoon/ evening/week) /ðɪs/

Verbs

believe /bɪ'liːv/
buy /baɪ/
die /daɪ/
follow /'fɒləʊ/
go to university /gəʊ tə ,juːnɪ'vɜːsəti/
leave /liːv/
organise /'ɔːgənaɪz/
protect /prə'tekt/
put up /pʊt 'ʌp/
remember /rɪ'membər/
snow /snəʊ/
tidy up /,taɪdi 'ʌp/
travel /'trævəl/
understand /,ʌndə'stænd/
work /wɜːk/

Nouns

conservation /,kɒnsə'veɪʃən/
coral reef /'kɒrəl riːf/
fish /fɪʃ/
hard work /hɑːd 'wɜːk/
information /,ɪnfə'meɪʃən/
money /'mʌni/
project /'prɒdʒekt/
research (n) /'rɪsɜːtʃ/
sea /siː/
television /'telɪvɪʒən/
volunteer /,vɒlən'tɪər/
world /wɜːld/

Adjectives

late /leɪt/

old /əʊld/
polluted /pə'luːtɪd/
ready /'redi/
terrible /'terəbl/
unhappy /ʌn'hæpi/
young /jʌŋ/

Everyday English

Check it out! /'tʃek ɪt 'aʊt/
Let's (follow her) /lets/
She must be crazy! /ʃi 'mʌst biː 'kreɪzi/
You're an angel! /jɔːr ən 'eɪndʒəl/

Unit 4

Articles and quantifiers

a/an /ə/, /æn/
a lot of /ə 'lɒt əv/
much/many /mʌtʃ/, /'meni/
some/any /sʌm/, /'eni/

Food, drink and meals

bacon and eggs (n) /'beɪkən ənd egz/
beef (n) /biːf/
bread (n) /bred/
breakfast (n) /'brekfəst/
calorie (n) /'kæləri/
carrot (n) /'kærət/
cereal (n) /'sɪərɪəl/
chicken (n) /'tʃɪkɪn/
curry (n) /'kʌri/
fish and chips (n) /fɪʃ ənd 'tʃɪps/
fried (adj) /fraɪd/
fruit juice (n) /'fruːt dʒuːs/
grapes (n) /greɪps/
grilled (adj) /grɪld/
hamburger (n) /'hæm,bɜːgər/
meal (n) /miːl/
meat (n) /miːt/
milk (n) /mɪlk/
mineral water (n) /'mɪnərəl ,wɔːtər/
mushroom (n) /'mʌʃrʊm/
omelette (n) /'ɒmlət/
onion (n) /'ʌnjən/
pasta (n) /'pæstə/
potato (n) /pə'teɪtəʊ/
restaurant (n) /'restrɒnt/
rice (n) /raɪs/
roast beef (n) /rəʊst 'biːf/
salad (n) /'sæləd/

sandwich (n) /'sænwɪdʒ/
sauce (n) /sɔːs/
seafood (n) /'siːfuːd/
snack (n) /snæk/
soup (n) /suːp/
sugar (n) /'ʃʊgər/
sweet (n) /swiːt/
take-away (n) /'teɪkəweɪ/
tea (n) /tiː/
toast (n) /təʊst/
tomato (n) /tə'mɑːtəʊ/
vegetable (n) /'vedʒtəbl/
waiter (n) /'weɪtər/
yoghurt (n) /'jɒgət/

Verbs

burn off /bɜːn 'ɒf/
exercise /'eksəsaɪz/
keep fit /kiːp 'fɪt/
order /'ɔːdər/
weigh /weɪ/

Adjectives

fit /fɪt/
healthy /'helθi/
overweight /'əʊvəweɪt/
unhealthy /ʌn'helθi/

Unit 5

Regular verbs

answer /'ɑːnsər/
attack /ə'tæk/
decide /dɪ'saɪd/
discover /dɪ'skʌvər/
kill /kɪl/
phone /fəʊn/
plan /plæn/
save /seɪv/
start /stɑːt/
stay /steɪ/
stop /stɒp/
tidy /'taɪdi/
try /traɪ/
visit /'vɪzɪt/

Phrasal verbs

climb down /klaɪm 'daʊn/
climb up /klaɪm 'ʌp/
come down /kʌm 'daʊn/
cut down /kʌt 'daʊn/
get in /get 'ɪn/
get out /get 'aʊt/
pick up /pɪk 'ʌp/
put down /pʊt 'daʊn/
put on /pʊt 'ɒn/
take off /teɪk 'ɒf/

Verbs

be born /biː 'bɔːn/

Nouns

company /'kʌmpəni/
dream /driːm/
environmental organisation
    /ɪn,vaɪrən'mentəl
    ,ɔːgənaɪ'zeɪʃən/
farmer /'fɑːmər/
firefighter /'faɪərfaɪtər/
forest /'fɒrɪst/
hero /'hɪərəʊ/
hospital /'hɒspɪtəl/
journey /'dʒɜːni/
medal /'medəl/
North Pole /nɔːθ 'pəʊl/
plan /plæn/
polar bear /'pəʊlər beər/
reporter /rɪ'pɔːtər/
tree /triː/
tree-house /'triːhaʊs/

Everyday English

loads of ... /'ləʊdz əv/
one day /'wʌn deɪ/
That's amazing.
    /ðæts ə'meɪzɪŋ/
You can't be serious.
    /juː 'kɑːnt biː 'sɪəriəs/

Unit 6

Past time expressions

(an hour/four days/ten
    years) ago /ə'gəʊ/
last (night/week/month/
    year) /lɑːst/
yesterday /'jestədeɪ/
yesterday morning
    (afternoon/evening)
    /,jestədeɪ 'mɔːnɪŋ/

Sports

athlete (n) /'æθliːt/
basketball (n)
    /'bɑːskɪtbɔːl/
cycling (n) /'saɪklɪŋ/
equipment (n)
    /ɪ'kwɪpmənt/
final (n) /'faɪnəl/
ice hockey (n) /aɪs 'hɒki/
long jump (n) /'lɒŋ dʒʌmp/
Olympic Games (n)
    /ə'lɪmpɪc geɪmz/
skateboarding (n)
    /'skeɪtbɔːdɪŋ/
skiing (n) /'skiːɪŋ/
snowboarding (n)
    /'snəʊbɔːdɪŋ/
surfing (n) /'sɜːfɪŋ/
swimming (n) /'swɪmɪŋ/

team (n) /tiːm/
volleyball (n) /'vɒlibɔːl/
water sport (n) /'wɔːtər
    spɔːt/

Verbs

ban /bæn/
beat /biːt/
begin /bɪ'gɪn/
call /kɔːl/
forget /fə'get/
get in touch with
    /get ɪn 'tʌtʃ wɪð/
go out with /gəʊ 'aʊt wɪð/
have an argument /hæv ən
    'ɑːgjumənt/
keep in touch with
    /kiːp ɪn 'tʌtʃ wɪð/
pour /pɔːr/
push /pʊʃ/
ring /rɪŋ/
send /send/
step /step/
take away /teɪk ə'weɪ/
take out /teɪk 'aʊt/
think /θɪŋk/
waste time /weɪst 'taɪm/
win /wɪn/

Nouns

cream cake /kriːm 'keɪk/
friendship /'frenʃɪp/
gold medal /gəʊld 'medəl/
present /'prezənt/
teenager /'tiːn,eɪdʒər/
text message/messaging
    /'tekst ,mesɪdʒ/
    /,mesɪdʒɪŋ/
winner /'wɪnər/

Adjectives

easy /'iːzi/
excellent /'eksələnt/
excited /ɪk'saɪtɪd/
popular /'pɒpjələr/
quick /kwɪk/
safe /seɪf/
short /ʃɔːt/
useful /'juːsfəl/

Unit 7

Jobs

business person (n)
    /'bɪznɪs ,pɜːsən/
computer programmer (n)
    /kəm,pjuːtər
    'prəʊgræmər/
dentist (n) /'dentɪst/
doctor (n) /'dɒktər/

engineer (n) /,endʒɪ'nɪər/
film star (n) /'fɪlm stɑːr/
flight attendant (n)
    /'flaɪt ə,tendənt/
lawyer (n) /'lɔɪər/
model (n) /'mɒdəl/
nurse (n) /nɜːs/
pilot (n) /'paɪlət/
policeman (n) /pə'liːsmən/
secretary (n) /'sekrətəri/
singer (n) /'sɪŋər/
sports person (n)
    /'spɔːts ,pɜːsən/
teacher (n) /'tiːtʃər/
tennis player (n)
    /'tenɪs ,pleɪər/
vet (n) /vet/
writer (n) /'raɪtər/

Verbs

be good at /biː 'gʊd ət/
have something in common
    /hæv ,sʌmθɪŋ ɪn
    'kɒmən/
have to /'hæv tuː/
look (perfect) /lʊk/
pull out (teeth) /pʊl aʊt/
share /ʃeər/
take exams /teɪk ɪg'zæmz/

Nouns

ability /ə'bɪləti/
talent /'tælənt/
washing machine
    /'wɒʃɪŋ mə,ʃiːn/

Adjectives

determined /dɪ'tɜːmɪnd/
famous /'feɪməs/
hard-working
    /,hɑːd'wɜːkɪŋ/
lucky /'lʌki/
necessary /'nesəsəri/
ordinary /'ɔːdənəri/
perfect /'pɜːfɪkt/
rich /rɪtʃ/
successful /sək'sesfəl/
sure /ʃʊər/

Everyday English

doing a paper round
    /,duːɪŋ ə 'peɪpə raʊnd/
hardly any (money)
    /,hɑːdli 'eni/
pocket money /'pɒkɪt
    ,mʌni/
save up /seɪv 'ʌp/

Unit 8

Sleep and dreams

asleep (adj) /əˈsliːp/
awake (adj) /əˈweɪk/
daydream (v, n) /ˈdeɪdriːm/
dream (v, n) /driːm/
get up (v) /get ˈʌp/
go to bed (v) /gəʊ tə ˈbed/
go to sleep (v) /gəʊ tə ˈsliːp/
wake up (v) /weɪk ˈʌp/

Verbs

change /tʃeɪndʒ/
continue /kənˈtɪnjuː/
create /kriˈeɪt/
criticise /ˈkrɪtɪsaɪz/

Nouns

audition /ɔːˈdɪʃən/
contest /ˈkɒntest/
contestant /kənˈtestənt/
conversation /ˌkɒnvəˈseɪʃn/
group /gruːp/
idea /aɪˈdɪə/
imagination /ɪˌmædʒɪˈneɪʃən/
inventor /ɪnˈventər/
judge /dʒʌdʒ/
painter /ˈpeɪntər/
paper /ˈpeɪpər/
pop idol /ˈpɒp ˌaɪdəl/
pop star /ˈpɒp staːr/
sand /sænd/
solo singer /ˈsəʊləʊ ˈsɪŋər/
songwriter /ˈsɒŋˌraɪtər/
talent show /ˈtælənt ʃəʊ/

Unit 9

Language learning

accent (n) /ˈæksənt/
communicate (v) /kəˈmjuːnɪkeɪt/
correct (v, adj) /kəˈrekt/
course (n) /kɔːs/
guess (v) /ges/
imitate (v) /ˈɪmɪteɪt/
look up (v) /lʊk ˈʌp/
make mistakes (v) /meɪk mɪˈsteɪks/
mean (v) /miːn/
mother tongue (n) /ˈmʌðə tʌŋ/
penfriend (n) /ˈpenfrend/
practise (v) /ˈpræktɪs/
pronounce (v) /prəˈnaʊns/

pronunciation (n) /prəˌnʌnsiˈeɪʃən/
speak (v) /spiːk/
translate (v) /trænzˈleɪt/
translation (n) /trænzˈleɪʃən/
wrong (adj) /rɒŋ/

Verbs

marry /ˈmaeri/

Adjectives

best /best/
better /ˈbetər/
boring /ˈbɔːrɪŋ/
cool /kuːl/
easy /ˈiːzi/
friendly /ˈfrendli/
further/farther /ˈfɜːðər/, /ˈfaːðər/
good-looking /ˌgʊdˈlʊkɪŋ/
handsome /ˈhænsəm/
important /ɪmˈpɔːtənt/
intelligent /ɪnˈtelɪdʒənt/
nice /naɪs/
normal /ˈnɔːməl/
popular /ˈpɒpjələr/
successful /səkˈsesfəl/
talented /ˈtæləntɪd/
unusual /ʌnˈjuːʒəl/
worse /wɜːs/

Everyday English

Ace! /eɪs/
Cool! /kuːl/
Groovy! /ˈgruːvi/
Hip! /hɪp/
Neat! /niːt/
Wicked! /ˈwɪkɪd/

Unit 10

Future time expressions

day after tomorrow /ˈdeɪ ˌaːftər təˌmɒrəʊ/
in three days' time /ɪn θriː deɪz taɪm/
next (week/Saturday) /nekst/
tomorrow /təˈmɒrəʊ/
week (month) after next /ˈwiːk aːftər nekst/

Holidays

activity (n) /ækˈtɪvəti/
adventure holiday (n) /ədˈventʃər ˈhɒlədeɪ/
backpack (n) /ˈbækpæk/

bed and breakfast (n) /bed ənd ˈbrekfəst/
camping (n) /ˈkæmpɪŋ/
campsite (n) /ˈkæmpsaɪt/
canal boat (n) /kəˈnæl bəʊt/
canoeing (n) /kəˈnuːɪŋ/
coach (n) /kəʊtʃ/
coast /kəʊst/
farm /faːm/
ferry (n) /ˈferi/
hiking (n) /ˈhaɪkɪŋ/
hire (v) /haɪər/
horse-riding (n) /ˈhɔːsraɪdɪŋ/
houseboat (n) /ˈhaʊsbəʊt/
island (n) /ˈaɪlənd/
kayak (n) /ˈkaɪæk/
mountain bike (n) /ˈmaʊntɪn baɪk/
nature (n) /ˈneɪtʃər/
on horseback (adv) /ɒn ˈhɔːsbæk/
postcard (n) /ˈpəʊskaːd/
sailing (n) /ˈseɪlɪŋ/
sightseeing (n) /ˈsaɪtsiːɪŋ/
snorkelling (n) /ˈsnɔːkəlɪŋ/
souvenir (n) /ˌsuːvənˈɪər/
summer camp (n) /ˈsʌmər kæmp/
sunbathing (n) /ˈsʌnbeɪðɪŋ/
surfboard (n) /ˈsɜːfbɔːd/
tourist (n) /ˈtɔːrɪst/
valley /ˈvæliː/
windsurfing (n) /ˈwɪndsɜːfɪŋ/
youth hostel (n) /ˈjuːθ ˌhɒstəl/

Unit 11

Verbs

crash /kræʃ/
float /fləʊt/
get married /get ˈmærid/
have children /hæv ˈtʃɪldrən/
relax /rɪˈlæks/

Nouns

bill /bɪl/
fortune cookie /ˈfɔːtʃuːn ˌkʊki/
galaxy /ˈgæləksi/
joke /dʒəʊk/
nonsense /ˈnɒnsəns/
planet /ˈplænɪt/
space /speɪs/
spaceship /ˈspeɪsʃɪp/
universe /ˈjuːnɪvɜːs/

Everyday English

Anything else? /ˌeniθɪŋ ˈels/
How embarassing! /ˌhaʊ ɪmˈbærəsɪŋ/
I don't believe it! /aɪ ˌdaʊnt bɪˈliːv ɪt/
(It's) nonsense /ˈnɒnsəns/
the best bit /ðə ˈbest bɪt/

Unit 12

The weather

avalanche (n) /ˈævəlaːnʃ/
cloudy (adj) /ˈklaʊdi/
foggy (adj) /ˈfɒgi/
hot /hɒt/
ice (n) /aɪs/
rain (n) /reɪn/
sunny (adj) /ˈsʌni/
warm (adj) /wɔːm/
windy (adj) /ˈwɪndi/

Verbs

break /breɪk/
give up /gɪv ˈʌp/
go on /gəʊ ˈɒn/
go wrong /gəʊ ˈrɒŋ/
hit /hɪt/
hope to /ˈhəʊp tʊ/
keep going /kiːp ˈgəʊɪŋ/
lift /lɪft/
reach /riːtʃ/
stand up /stænd ˈʌp/
strengthen /ˈstreŋθən/

Nouns

climber /ˈklaɪmər/
determination /dɪˌtɜːmɪˈneɪʃən/
immigrant /ˈɪmɪgrənt/
painting /ˈpeɪntɪŋ/
politics /ˈpɒlətɪks/
rope /rəʊp/

Adverbs

badly /ˈbædli/
bitterly (cold) /ˈbɪtəli/
carefully /ˈkeəfəli/
fast /faːst/
gradually /ˈgrædʒuəli/
hard /haːd/
heavily /ˈhevɪli/
loudly /ˈlaʊdli/
luckily /ˈlʌkɪli/
quietly /ˈkwaɪətli/
slowly /ˈsləʊli/
well /wel/

Unit 13

Celebrations

birthday cake (n) /'bɜːθdeɪ keɪk/
celebrate (v) /'seləbreɪt/
fireworks (n) /'faɪəwɜːks/
New Year's Eve (Day) (n) /njuː jɪəʳz 'iːv/

Phrasal verbs

fall off /fɔːl 'ɒf/
get across /get ə'krɒs/
give up (smoking) /gɪv ʌp/
go off /gəʊ 'ɒf/
go on /gəʊ 'ɒn/
keep up /kiːp 'ʌp/
stick to /'stɪk tuː/
take up /teɪk 'ʌp/
throw away /θrəʊ ə'weɪ/
work out (a problem) /wɜːk aʊt/

Verbs

be going to /biː 'gəʊɪŋ tuː/
have a shower /hæv ə 'ʃaʊəʳ/
must /mʌst/
record /re'kɔːd/

Nouns

resolution /ˌrezə'luːʃən/

Unit 14

Verbs

bow /baʊ/
kiss /kɪs/
reply /rɪ'plaɪ/
should /ʃʊd/
touch /tʌtʃ/

Nouns

custom /'kʌstəm/
leather /'leðəʳ/
queue /kjuː/
tip /tɪp/

Adjectives of personality

cheerful /'tʃɪəfəl/
dishonest /dɪ'sɒnɪst/
disorganised /dɪs'ɔːgənaɪzd/
dull /dʌl/
friendly /'frendli/
funny /'fʌni/
hard-working /ˌhɑːd'wɜːkɪŋ/
honest /'ɒnɪst/
kind /kaɪnd/
lazy /'leɪzi/
miserable /'mɪzərəbl/
nervous /'nɜːvəs/
organised /'ɔːgənaɪzd/
relaxed /rɪ'lækst/
rude /ruːd/
unfriendly /ʌn'frendli/
unkind /ʌn'kaɪnd/

Adjectives of opinion

attractive /ə'træktɪv/
awful /'ɔːfəl/
brilliant /'brɪliənt/
boring /'bɔːrɪŋ/
dreadful /'dredfəl/
interesting /'ɪntrəstɪŋ/
ugly /'ʌgli/

Unit 15

Verbs

ask somebody out /ɑːsk ˌsʌmbədi 'aʊt/
burn /bɜːn/
can't stand /kɑːnt 'stænd/
collapse /kə'læps/
drop /drɒp/
feel /fiːl/
frighten /'fraɪtən/
keep calm /kiːp 'kɑːm/
might /maɪt/
overturn /ˌəʊvət3ːn/
recognise /'rekəgnaɪz/
show /ʃəʊ/

Nouns

danger /'deɪndʒəʳ/
gorilla /gə'rɪlə/
gun /gʌn/
shark /ʃɑːk/
situation /ˌsɪtju'eɪʃən/

Compound nouns

bank robber /'bæŋk ˌrɒbəʳ/
firefighter /'faɪəʳˌfaɪtəʳ/
mountain climber /'maʊntɪn ˌklaɪməʳ/
parachute jumper /'pærəʃuːt ˌdʒʌmpəʳ/
racing driver /'reɪsɪŋ ˌdraɪvəʳ/
underwater photographer /ˌʌndəwɔːtəʳ fə'tɒgrəfəʳ/

Adjectives of feeling

annoyed /ə'nɔɪd/
annoying /ə'nɔɪɪŋ/
bored /bɔːʳd/
brave /breɪv/
calm /kɑːm/
excited /ɪk'saɪtɪd/
exciting /ɪk'saɪtɪŋ/
frightened /'fraɪtənd/
frightening /'fraɪtənɪŋ/
interested /'ɪntrəstɪd/
interesting /'ɪntrəstɪŋ/
terrified /'terəfaɪd/
tired /taɪəʳd/
tiring /'taɪərɪŋ/

Everyday English

Hang on. /hæŋ 'ɒn/
How should I know? /haʊ ʃəd 'aɪ nəʊ/
No big deal. /'nəʊ bɪg 'diːl/
No way! /nəʊ 'weɪ/

Unit 16

Animals

alligator (n) /'ælɪgeɪtəʳ/
cow (n) /kaʊ/
frog (n) /frɒg/
mouse (n) /maʊs/
parrot (n) /'pærət/
rabbit (n) /'ræbɪt/
snake (n) /sneɪk/
tarantula (n) /tə'ræntjələ/
tiger (n) /'taɪgəʳ/

Verbs

bite /baɪt/
collect /kə'lekt/
complain /kəm'pleɪn/
seem /siːm/

Verb + noun pairs

break a record /breɪk ə 'rekɔːd/
build a house /bɪld ə 'haʊs/
raise money /reɪz 'mʌni/
take a risk /teɪk ə 'rɪsk/
tell a joke /tel ə 'dʒəʊk/
win a prize /wɪn ə 'praɪz/

Nouns

album /'ælbəm/
anniversary /ˌænɪ'vɜːsəri/
charity /'tʃærɪti/
collection /kə'lekʃən/
death /deθ/
escape /ɪ'skeɪp/
fan /fæn/
fingernail /'fɪŋgəneɪl/
ghost /gəʊst/
head /hed/
hit /hɪt/
look-alike /'lʊkəlaɪk/
neighbour /'neɪbəʳ/
record /'rekɔːd/
sighting /'saɪtɪŋ/
sky-diver /'skaɪˌdaɪvəʳ/
wheelchair /'wiːltʃeəʳ/
world record /wɜːld 'rekɔːd/

Adjectives

mad /mæd/
middle-aged /ˌmɪdl'eɪdʒd/
poor /pɔːʳ/

Thanks and acknowledgements

The authors would like to thank a number of people whose support proved invaluable at various stages of the planning, writing and production process of *English in Mind*:

Peter Donovan for inviting us do this exciting project for Cambridge University Press; Angela Lilley, Publishing Director at Cambridge University Press, for her leadership abilities and the support we got from her; James Dingle, our commissioning editor, for his commitment to the project, and for managing the editorial team; Annabel Marriott for her enthusiasm, her many excellent ideas and her commitment to quality in the editing of this course; Jackie McKillop for steering the course through its production.

The teenage students we have taught over the years who have posed interesting challenges and who in many ways have become teachers for us; the teachers we have met in staff rooms, workshops and seminars in many countries who have shared their insights and asked questions that became guidelines in our own search for excellence in teaching teenagers.

A number of authors whose writings have been important for us in giving shape to the thinking behind *English in Mind*: Kieran Egan, for his valuable insights into the psychology of the teenage student that have helped us enormously to find the right content for the books; Howard Gardner, Robert Dilts and Earl Stevick, for helping us understand more about the wonders of the human mind; Mihaly Csikszentmihalyi , for his insights into the flow state, without which our own work would have been much less enjoyable.

The team at Pentacor Book Design for giving the book its design; Anne Rosenfeld for the audio recordings; Meredith Levy, Hilary Ratcliff, Annie Cornford, Fran Banks and Ruth Pellegrini for their excellent editorial support; and all other people involved in creating this course.

Last, but not least we would like to thank our partners, Mares and Adriana, for their support.

The authors and publishers would like to thank the teachers who commented on the material at different stages of its development:

Belgium: Chantal Alexandrer; Marie-Christine Callaert; David Collie; Myriam Deplechin; Denise De Vleeschauwer; Claude Hallett; Valerie Hirsoux; Marie-Louise Leujeune Claes; Ingrid Quix; Cecile Rouffiange Donckers; Bruno Tremault; Edithe van Eycke; Patrick Verheyen; Jan Vermeiren. Italy: Elena Assirelli; Gloria Gaiba; Grazia Maria Niccolaioni; Deanna Serantoni Donatini; Cristiana Ziraldo. Poland: Malgorzata Dyszlewska; Ewa Paciorek; Julita Moninska; Pawel Morawski; Dorota Muszynska; Switzerland: Irena Engelmann; Niki Low; Susan Ann Sell.

We would also like to thank all the teachers who allowed us to observe their classes, and who gave up their valuable time for interviews and focus groups.

The publishers are grateful to Onward Music Ltd (Bucks Music Group) for permission to reproduce the lyrics to *Space Oddity* by David Bowie on page 93, and to Marathon Music International Limited, www.mmiuk.com, for the sound recording, © Marathon Music.

The publishers are grateful to the following for permission to reproduce photographic material:

Art Director's and Trip pp. 44(m), 64(b), 86(b); Camera Press pp. 62(e), 62(f), 72–73(t); Corbis pp. 8(b), 9(mr), 13(a), 13(b), 13(c), 13(e), 21(6), 49(3), 49(4), 49(5), 50, 53(l), 56(br), 57, 62(a), 62(b), 62(c), 62(d), 64(I), 64(j), 77(5), 80, 84(tr), 84(b), 88(b), 95, 96, 100-101, 121(2), 121(4), 128(b); Eye Ubiquitous p. 86(m); Getty Images pp. 8(a), 8(c), 8(d), 9(l), 9(ml), 9(r), 12(g), 13(d), 13(f), 13(g), 13(h), 21(4), 21(5), 22, 34, 44(tl), 44(bl), 45(tl), 64(a), 64(c), 64(d), 64(e), 64(f), 64(g), 64(h), 77(6), 79, 84(tl), 84(mr), 86(t), 88(t), 89(r) 92, 93, 104(2), 105(5), 106(tr), 112, 121(1), 121(3), 121(5), 128(l), 128-129(m), 129(r); Hulton Getty p. 56(tr): Impact Photos pp. 77(4), 78; Network Photographers p. 45(bl); Powerstock p. 31; Rex Features pp. 12(b), 20(2), 28, 30, 40, 48(2), 53(r), 72(bl), 72-73(br), 105(3), 105(4), 124(a), 124(c); Chris Ridley pp. 49(7), 65; Helen Thayer pp. 55; Topham pp. 77(3), 84(ml), 89(l); Zooid Pictures pp. 124(b), 124(e).

All other photographs taken by Gareth Boden.

The publishers are grateful to the following illustrators:

Dan Alexander, c/o Advocate Illustration pp. 6, 24, 36, 58, 108; Kate Charlesworth p. 116; Yane Christensen, c/o Advocate Illustration pp. 9, 19, 59, 107, 113, 133; Mark Duffin pp. 10, 11, 69, 90, 117, 134, 136; Mandy Greatorex, c/o New Division pp. 15, 18, 41, 43, 112; Sophie Joyce pp. 14, 17, 42, 70, 85, 98; Ken Oliver, c/o Wildlife Art p. 118; Peters & Zabransky pp. 4, 8, 28, 29, 78, 98; David Shenton pp. 19, 24, 52, 83, 88, 97, 109, 120, 125, 127; Kim Smith, c/o Eastwing Illustration Agency pp. 5, 16, 17, 35, 132, 135; Kath Walker pp. 16, 23, 37, 53, 63, 95, 97, 109, 120; Darrell Warner, c/o Beehive Illustration pp. 14, 25, 37, 56, 71, 87, 99, 125; Stuart Williams, c/o The Organisation pp. 7, 27, 39, 45, 67, 73, 89, 101, 123;

The publishers are grateful to the following for their assistance with commissioned photographs: Parkside Community College, Cambridge; Christ's School, Richmond, London; The Jackie Palmer Agency.

The publishers are grateful to the following contributors:

Gareth Boden: commissioned photography
Meredith Levy: editorial work
Ruth Pellegrini: permissions research, wordlist compilation
Pentacor Book Design: text design and layouts
Hilary Ratcliff: editorial work
Anne Rosenfeld: audio recordings
Sally Smith: photographic direction, picture research
Tim Wharton: music and recording of the song on page 70